THE SERMONS OF RICHARD HOOKER

PHILIP SECOR is a leading authority on the life and thought of Richard Hooker. His acclaimed biography, *Richard Hooker Prophet of Anglicanism* (Burns & Oates/Anglican Book Centre, 1999), along with numerous recent articles and hundreds of sermons and talks in Anglican and Episcopal churches, have helped to awaken a broad interest in the founding theologian of the Anglican tradition.

It is especially appropriate that Dr Secor should make available this first modern edition of Hooker's sermons during the 400th anniversary year of Hooker's death. In so doing, he has made Hooker's timeless legacy more readily available to Christians in the twenty-first century.

Secor holds his BA from Drew University and his MA and PhD from Duke University. He has taught at Duke, Dickinson College and Davidson College and been Dean of the College at Muhlenberg College and President of Cornell College. He lives with his wife, Anne, in eastern Pennsylvania, USA.

THE SERMONS OF RICHARD HOOKER

THE POWER OF FAITH, THE MYSTERY OF GRACE

A Modern Edition

Philip B. Secor

First published in Great Britain 2001
Society for Promoting Christian Knowledge
Holy Trinity Church
Marylebone Road
London NW1 4DU

ACKNOWLEDGEMENTS

Unless otherwise stated Biblical quotations are from *The New English Bible* © 1961, 1970, 2001 Oxford and Cambridge University Presses.

British Library Cataloguing-in-Publication Data

A catalogue record for this book is available from the British Library

ISBN 0-281-05414-2

Typeset by FiSH Books, London
Printed in Great Britain by Mackays of Chatham

Contents

For
W. Speed Hill

Preface

Richard Hooker is usually regarded as the formative theologian of the Church of England and of the worldwide Anglican Communion, which today numbers some seventy million souls living and worshipping in every corner of the globe. Some have called Hooker the 'prophet' of Anglicanism and the closest counterpart in the English Reformation to Luther and Calvin.[1]

Hooker was born about Easter 1554 in the village of Heavitree, just outside the walls of the ancient cathedral city of Exeter. His life spanned the reigns of two monarchs whose impact on Church affairs was decisive: Mary Tudor, who sought to restore Roman Catholicism and the Pope's authority to England following the Protestant reforms of her brother Edward VI's reign, and Elizabeth I, who was to unify Church and State in a moderately reformed and inclusive Christian commonwealth. It was to be Hooker's role to explain and defend in timeless language the style and form of that reformed Church that would one day be called 'Anglican'.

The young Hooker excelled in grammar school and went up to Corpus Christi College, Oxford, under the patronage of the famed Bishop of Salisbury, John Jewel. While there he completed his BA and MA, was ordained, and became the tutor to a number of prominent young men including Edwin Sandys, son of the Archbishop of York, and George Cranmer, great-nephew of Archbishop Thomas Cranmer. Archbishop Sandys was so pleased with Hooker's work with his son that he convinced the Queen to appoint Hooker to the important post of Master of the Temple Church in London. This church, regularly attended by the lawyers and judges at the Inns of Court, had become a centre for the more radical elements of Calvinist theology and Presbyterian liturgy and polity that Elizabeth was trying to suppress. Hooker was to be her champion as he preached each Sunday morning a more moderate and inclusive brand of Calvinism. Each Sunday afternoon, his sermons were refuted by his assistant, Walter Travers, a Reader at the church and an arch-Calvinist. Thus unfolded what I call in my biography of Hooker, 'The Great Debate of the English Reformation'. The most important and influential sermons of Hooker's career were preached during these years (1584–92). Parts of them are extant and are included in this volume.

While at the Temple Hooker roomed at the nearby house of John Churchman, a prominent London merchant. In 1588, the year of the Spanish Armada, the 34-year-old Hooker married Churchman's daughter, Joan, a young woman of about 21. They were to have six children, but only one survived beyond the age of 21. By 1590, Hooker was hard at work on the defining task of his life. This was his great treatise, *Of the Laws of Ecclesiastical Polity*, the timeless explanation and *apologia* of Anglicanism. The book was published in stages over many years: the first four books in 1593, the fifth, and most important, in 1597, and the balance posthumously in 1648 and 1662.

To spare him the hectic life of Master of the Temple, the Queen relieved him of that post in 1591 and granted him a largely absentee appointment as a minor canon at Salisbury Cathedral and rector of the nearby parish of Boscombe. In 1595, she gave him the well-endowed country parish at Bishopsbourne in Kent, just down the road from Canterbury Cathedral. Here he ministered quietly to his flock and completed his writings. He died on 3 November 1600. Almost immediately thereafter his fame began to spread and for centuries he remained the most important figure in Anglican thought.

In recent years, however, Hooker has been largely unknown outside a small group of professional historians and theologians and a scattering of clerics and informed Christians, mostly Anglicans, Episcopalians, and Roman Catholics. Now, as we celebrate the 400th anniversary of his death, in November 2000, there has been renewed interest in his life and works, reflected in a recently completed authoritative edition of his works and a new biography.[2]

Scholars dispute whether Hooker's *Laws* is the most important *apologia* for Anglicanism, a prophetic work on which later theologians and churchmen built that tradition, or a political polemic designed to protect the emerging Anglican Church from its enemies, primarily radical Calvinists of the separatist and Puritan stamp. It is all of these and something more – a source of inspiration and a guidebook for generations of Anglican and Episcopalian church leaders seeking to understand and apply their unique style of worship and Christian living. True, this is expressed and reflected above all in *The Book of Common Prayer*, which was principally compiled and written by Archbishop Thomas Cranmer. But it was Hooker, not Cranmer, who explained how God's will could be known, why the Prayer Book enjoined all the special features of worship and liturgical experience that it did, and how Anglicans were to express their faith in the world.

The theological and liturgical legacy of Hooker to Anglicans and Episcopalians, including all those millions who do not know his name and certainly have not read his massive theological treatise, has been almost inestimable. Yet Hooker has still more to give to his Church. This comes in the form of his more intimate and personal wisdom as expressed not through theological writings but through sermons, lectures and shorter tractates. These inspiring pieces, not always completely coherent or internally consistent and in some cases only fragmentary as they come down to us, have never been truly accessible to the contemporary general reader. It is the purpose of this volume to remedy that defect and allow Hooker to speak to a new generation of clerical and lay Christians in the voice of pastor, teacher and fellow churchman.[3]

Though he is better known to posterity as a theologian, most of Hooker's career was that of priest of the church: pastor, teacher and preacher. He was ordained in 1579 while a fellow at Corpus Christi College, Oxford. During his two decades as a priest (he in fact preferred the term 'presbyter') he preached from at least half a dozen pulpits, probably more. He served two churches as the resident minister: the Temple Church in London from 1585 to 1591, and St Mary's in Bishopsbourne, Kent from 1595 until his death in 1600. He also preached from the pulpits of St Mary's in Drayton

Beauchamp, Oxfordshire (1584) and St Andrew's, Boscombe, near Salisbury (1591–95), where he served as rector on at least a part-time basis. He probably also preached from time to time at Oxford, at Salisbury Cathedral, and possibly at the churches of his in-laws, the Churchmans: St Augustine's in London and St Andrew's in Enfield. A turning point in Hooker's career was his sermon in 1584 at Paul's Cross, the famous open-air pulpit in St Paul's churchyard in London. To be selected to preach in such a prestigious pulpit, before many of the leading religious and political figures of the realm, was a high honour, signalling Hooker's rise in the Church. Not long after this sermon, in which he cautioned against extreme Calvinist views of predestination (damnation and 'election'), Hooker was appointed to serve as Master of the Temple Church.

In the process of working with Hooker's sermons I have discovered an unmistakable theme running through them all which I call 'the power of faith and the mystery of grace'. Whatever topic he may be discussing – justice, sorrow, fear, depression, sin, joy, doubt, prayer, the Church, the Sacraments, heresy, salvation, prophecy, Roman Catholics – he persistently grounds his explanations and his exhortations in the efficacy of faith to unlock and unleash the unfathomable glory of God's mercy in Christ.

To present Hooker's sermons in contemporary English is a perilous task, one requiring courage in the editor/translator and trust in the reader. It is a perilous task because Hooker's language, though often too antiquated and disjointed to carry his meaning to the modern mind, is arranged in a form which is carefully contrived to achieve definite rhetorical effect and hence must be altered only with great delicacy. Courage in the editor/translator is demanded because to tamper with Hooker's language is to invade one of the most important and carefully guarded texts in western literature. Faith by the reader is necessary because she or he is unlikely ever to consult the difficult original texts to verify the integrity and sagacity of the translator.

A word about this word, 'translator'. Years of living daily with the words (and ideas) of Hooker have convinced me that what is involved in putting his thoughts into the idiom of contemporary

English is nothing less than a decision, sometimes word by word and sentence by sentence, about how best to express his words in phrases that will be intelligible to the contemporary reader without losing the meaning, which is so often captured in the syntax and rhetorical constructions of the sentences. The answer in the first instance is, of course, to change as little as possible. This has been my goal as I approached each new thought of Hooker's. I have followed the original as closely as possible, presenting almost everything in the text and preserving, wherever possible, Hooker's style. This means that where Hooker's prose is disjointed, unclear or incoherent and where his transitions are weak, my rendition will reflect these problems. It is no part of my intention to make Hooker say what he did not say in order to make him look better.

Often I have found it necessary to go beyond paraphrase and 'translate' (there is no other word for it) Hooker's thought into revised sentences which can provide for the modern reader both the bare meaning intended by Hooker and the rhetorical thrust which is so vital to grasping his full spirit. It has also been necessary to omit altogether an occasional passage that seems redundant or obscure. I have done these things only when I thought it absolutely necessary and have almost always retained without alteration the special pithy phrases and wonderful aphorisms that punctuate Hooker's style.[4]

To show why a new edition of the sermons is necessary to make them attractive to most contemporary readers, and to illustrate my method, here are three examples:

From the *First Sermon Upon Part of St Jude's Epistle*

Hooker's text (Folger Edition)	*This edition*
The occasion whereupon, together with the end whereof, this Epistle was written, is opened in the front and entire of the same. (p. 13)	Both the occasion and the purpose of St Jude are clearly opened to our understanding at the outset and throughout the entire Epistle.

From *A Learned Discourse of Justification . . .*

God rewardeth abundantly every one which worketh yett not for any meritorious dignity which is or can be in the works but through His mere mercie by whose comaundmente He worketh. (p. 160)	God abundantly rewards everyone who does good works, not for any value in the works themselves, but solely because of His mercy.

From *A Learned Sermon of the Nature of Pride*

Only men in all their actions know what it is they seek for, neither are they by any such necessity tyed naturally unto any certain determinate mean to obtein their end by but that they may if they will foresake it. (p. 311)	Only humans, in all their actions, know what it is they seek and are not bound by any predetermined means to achieve those ends.

I need to make special note of a few significant liberties taken with Hooker's texts. First, there is the matter of the personal pronoun. Usually I have retained Hooker's almost exclusive use of the masculine pronoun. But whenever I thought it would not violate Hooker's intent or the historical context, I have, in the spirit of our day, tried to welcome female readers into Hooker's audience by the use of more inclusive pronouns.

Secondly, I have abandoned both the titles and the chronology given to Hooker's sermons by earlier editors. Because my purpose is to interest as wide an audience as possible in what Hooker has to say, I have created new titles which are more suggestive of the content of the sermons and have arranged them in a thematic manner that I trust will make them more accessible and useful.

Thirdly, I have given (at the end of each sermon) Hooker's references to Scripture, something he did not usually do himself. His knowledge of Scripture was so deep and unselfconscious that he simply wove biblical references into his narrative with partial quotations and paraphrases. He usually used the *Geneva Bible* (1560). On those few occasions when I have felt it necessary to provide a more modern citation I have used the *New English Bible* (1970).[5]

Finally, I should clarify the word 'sermon'. Strictly speaking, not all of the works appearing in this volume are what most of us would call sermons, that is, compositions delivered from a pulpit, probably from memory or with the aid of a few notes. In Hooker's day there were, in addition to sermons in this sense, also polished lectures read from the pulpit and treatises (or tractates) on religious subjects that were written to be read privately and not usually spoken aloud from a pulpit.

Of the ten surviving pieces from Hooker, three were clearly prepared and delivered as sermons (*A Remedy Against Sorrow and Fear* and the two *Jude* sermons); one was a tractate, probably not delivered from a pulpit (*Of the Nature of Pride*), one was a tractate that was delivered from a pulpit (*Discourse of Justification . . .*), and the others were probably lectures delivered orally in church.[6]

This has been for the most part a solitary enterprise, save for the ever-present company of my wise friend Richard Hooker. Still, there are a few people to thank. They include my friend, wife, and steady supporter, Anne Secor, and the Hooker scholar nonpareil, W. Speed Hill, general editor of the authoritative *Folger Library Edition of the Works of Richard Hooker*, to whom I happily dedicate this work. Dr Hill has spent much of his professional life studying Hooker's texts and supervising the *Folger Edition* which is, without doubt, the most important contribution to Hooker studies in a century, a gigantic undertaking to which he has himself been a major contributor. He has provided many helpful suggestions for this work. Without the careful textual scholarship and helpful commentaries of Laetitia Yeandle and Egil Grislis in Volume V of the *Folger Edition*, I would not have had a reliable text on which to base this work. I am also grateful to another editor of the *Folger Edition*, the distinguished Canadian scholar of the English

Renaissance and Reformation, P. G. Stanwood, who has critiqued several of the sermons and given me important suggestions for making this book more useful to the reader. Finally, I thank Joanna Moriarty at SPCK for shepherding this work through to publication and, most especially, for providing me with a superb editor in Joanne Hill. Ms Hill's intelligent, sensitive and careful examination of each line and thought in a difficult manuscript has substantially improved the accuracy of my rendering of Hooker's sermons.

But, at the end of the day, most of the joy in this work and all of the blame for its shortcomings are mine.

Hellertown, Pennsylvania
2 November 2000 (the 400th anniversary of Richard Hooker's death)

Notes

1. See Philip B. Secor, *Richard Hooker Prophet of Anglicanism* (Burns & Oates, Tunbridge Wells; The Anglican Book Centre, Toronto, 1999); David L. Edwards, *Christianity: The First Two Thousand Years* (Cassell, London, 1997), 326.
2. W. Speed Hill, gen. ed., *The Folger Library Edition of the Works of Richard Hooker* Vols I–V (The Belknap Press of Harvard University, Cambridge, MA and London, 1977–1990); Vols VI–VII (Medieval & Renaissance Texts and Studies, Binghamton, NY and Tempe, Arizona, 1993–1998); Secor, *Richard Hooker*.
3. Seven of Hooker's sermons and tracts were included in John Keble's edition of Hooker's works: *The Works of Mr. Richard Hooker*, 7th edn (Oxford University Press, Oxford, 1887), Vol. III, 469–547, 597–709. The definitive edition of the sermons and tracts is by Laetitia Yeandle of the Folger Shakespeare Library and her editorial colleague, Egil Grislis, in Volume V of the *Folger Edition*. Without their work, I would never have attempted this paraphrase and 'translation' into contemporary English.
4. Some Hooker scholars may not appreciate my taking such liberties, just as a few did not appreciate my attempt to 'humanize' Hooker in my recent biography. I can only hope that scholars will understand that I intend no disrespect. I too prefer Hooker in the 'original'. My interest is to make Hooker's great wisdom available to a much wider audience than is possible by strict adherence to a text that is much too taxing for all but a few people. A well-expressed contrary view will be found in a recent work on Hooker's thought by the outstanding Hooker authority, John Booty. See his excellent *Reflections on the Theology of Richard Hooker* (The University of the South Press, Sewanee, TN, 1998), 3, 209.

5. I follow these rules in selecting upper or lower case for pronouns referring to the Deity: (1) when speaking in my own voice as editor, I capitalize the pronouns referring to God or Christ; (2) when I quote from the NEB, I follow its usage; (3) when I reproduce Hooker's Bible quotations (usually from the *Geneva Bible*) I follow his usage; (4) where Hooker is not quoting directly from Scripture, I translate his pronouns in the upper case.
6. See P. E. Forte, 'Richard Hooker as Preacher', *Folger Edition*, V, 663–6.

Proem

In recent years Anglicans have begun to wake up to the fact that they have a largely undiscovered theological heritage. The writings of Richard Hooker were formative for Anglicanism and have been studied by theologians for the past four centuries. They can still wonderfully inspire and inform our Christian reflection and prayer. We need more of Hooker's strong, calm, cultured spirituality. His great work, *Of the Laws of Ecclesiastical Polity*, can still help us to know who we are as a Church and a Communion. But somehow Hooker's thought has not reached most of the clergy or thoughtful lay Anglicans.

There are good (as well as not so good) reasons for that neglect. Hooker's style is highly distinctive, perhaps unique, and certainly difficult. He is hard going until one gets acclimatized. Although Hooker was once translated into Latin, he cannot be simply paraphrased. Something more than paraphrase is needed if Hooker is to speak to twenty-first-century people.

Philip Secor's devotion to Hooker is second to none and he has done much to bring Hooker and his struggles to life, on both sides of the Atlantic, with his recent biography, *Richard Hooker Prophet of Anglicanism*. Now he helps to make Hooker's sermons readable and understood in prose that is clear, robust and tinged with pathos, where that is appropriate. Secor's project may perhaps trouble some purists, but it is not, of course, intended to replace the original text. It brings Hooker nearer to us and anything that does that is to be encouraged. Hooker has so much to offer us still. In mediating Hooker to new generations, Secor's project has integrity.

The collection includes an extract from Hooker's great discourse on the doctrine of Justification. This has enormous relevance in the light of the report of the Anglican–Roman Catholic International Commission's report, *Salvation and the Church* (which still has to be fully received by the Anglican Communion) and the important recent Roman Catholic–Lutheran Joint Declaration on the same issue.

I wonder whether Secor could be persuaded to give the crucial Book V of the Ecclesiastical Polity the same sensitive treatment he has given the sermons?

The Revd Dr Paul Avis
General Secretary, Council for Christian Unity
of the Church of England
Director, Centre for the Study of the Christian Church

Foreword

Richard Hooker's theology of preaching is profound and expressed with clarity. In essence, preaching is the proclamation of 'heavenlie mysteries', and therefore a means of grace. With eloquence and enthusiasm, Hooker celebrates preaching 'as the blessed ordinance of God' and sermons 'as keyes to the kingdom of heaven, as winges to the soul, as spurs to the good affections of man . . .' Yet there is an all-too-human side to all preaching, since the preacher relies on his own wisdom as he applies God's truth to human need. Inevitably, at times some sermons proceed not from wisdom but from a 'corrupt fountain'. Hooker's careful and threefold appeal to Scripture, tradition and reason decreases the risk of error, but does not exclude it. Ultimately, acknowledges Hooker, all human 'skill in preaching is God's good gift'.

Repeatedly confronted by the Puritan dissidents, Hooker expanded the concept of preaching to include both the inspired writing and the public reading of Scripture, as well as the public reading of written sermons. Hooker argues: '. . . what is there in the best of sermons being offered, which they loose by being read?' But did Hooker actually read his own sermons? The most prejudiced tradition from the seventeenth century has been repeated often. And to anyone who has struggled with Hooker's prose, the report of Thomas Fuller might seem plausible:

> Mr Hooker . . . his voice was low, stature little, gesture none at all, standing stone-still in the Pulpit, as if the posture of his body were the emblem of his minde, unmovable in his opinions. Where his eye was left fixed at the beginning, it was found fixed at the end of his sermon. In a word, the doctrine he delivered had nothing but itself to garnish it. His stile was long and pithy, driving on a whole flock of several clauses before he came to the close of a sentence.

As recently noted by Philip Secor, the other side of the story should not be overlooked. Having severely criticized, indeed caricatured Hooker, Thomas Fuller describes the preaching style of his Puritan opponent Walter Travers in most glowing terms: 'Mr. Travers' utterance was graceful, gesture plausible, matter profitable, method plain, and his style carried with it *indolem pietatis*, "a genius of grace" flowing from the sanctified heart.'

Now while the sermons of Walter Travers are not available, his several books are. I will have to confess that I have read them with care, but found them colourless and lacking theological depth. Fuller, by inordinately praising Walter Travers, has significantly undermined the credibility of his description of Hooker – which is not to deny that there were serious problems with the prose of Hooker's sermons! In appreciation of Hooker, it can be noted that in the last analysis his brilliance has a way of revealing his depth. W. Speed Hill has called attention to Hooker's remarkable capacity for involving the reader existentially in a most personal way: 'We may posit three sources', says Hill, 'peculiar to Hooker himself: First, the brilliance and ease with which he manipulates scholastic dialect; second, the intensively personal and humane character of his use of Scripture; and third, the capacity to reach out, beyond dialectic and citation, to the experience of his auditors and to depict, by means of a gift for metaphor and a sense of tone, to an entire spectrum of man's spiritual life.'

And yet, there is a sense in which Hooker himself obscured what he had to say. His style, somewhat difficult in his own time, became increasingly more difficult. Hence the celebration of this new and exquisitely beautiful translation acknowledges an authentically felt need. Let me put this in personal terms and point to a parallel. If in my graduate school days in the early 1950s the most often quoted biblical text was the King James version of 1611, today it is seldom being heard in public. Several contemporary versions have gained an undisputed priority. Their clarity and beauty are responsible for their popularity and hence authority. Philip Secor's edition – indeed, translation – of Hooker's sermons has accomplished a similar task. Unobscured and deeply moving,

Hooker speaks again. He speaks wisely and clearly, and can move the reader deeply. I believe that in this new edition Richard Hooker will bring spiritual joy to a new generation of readers.

The Revd Egil Grislis
Professor of Religion, University of Manitoba
and co-editor, *The Folger Library Edition of the Works of Richard Hooker*

— 1 —
Faith and Doubt[1]

✵

This sermon, bearing the title, 'A Learned and Comfortable Sermon of the Certainty and Perpetuity of Faith in the Elect', was delivered at the Temple Church in London in 1585 and first published in 1612. It is one of several that precipitated Hooker's controversy with the renowned Presbyterian Calvinist, Walter Travers, and launched his career as a major apologist for the emergent Anglicanism that would characterize the Church of England in the next century. Along with several other tractates, known collectively as 'A Learned Discourse Of Justification . . .', that were delivered early in his tenure as Master of the Temple Church, this one was immortalized by Thomas Fuller in his History of the Worthies of England, *when he wrote of it and of Travers' response that 'the Pulpit spake pure Canterbury in the morning and Geneva in the afternoon . . .'*[2]

In this sermon, Hooker addresses the timeless problem for Christians of how to maintain their faith in the face of the doubt and despair produced by their human condition. His response is a powerful affirmation of the 'certainty' and 'perpetuity' of faith.

The text for the sermon, Habakkuk 1.4, was used because it spoke to the violent, intemperate and often confused state of affairs in the England of his day.

> ***Devastation and violence confront me; strife breaks out, discord raises its head, and so law grows effete; justice does not come forth victorious; for the wicked outwit the righteous, and so justice comes out perverted.*** Habakkuk 1.4 (NEB)[3]

— *On Evidence, Reason, and Faith* —

Does the prophet Habakkuk, in admitting the idea into his mind that God's law has failed, show himself to be an unbeliever?

We have seen in my earlier sermons on this text, first, what the objects of faith are; second, why it is that all men do not have strong faith; third, why it is that those who keep their faith often do so despite small assurance of any reward for doing so.

Because it is so easy to distort and misconstrue the truest of statements and because the smallest error can endanger our understanding, I will elaborate further on the third question of why some people are able to keep their faith in the face of great threats to it. Then I will proceed to my fourth point, which is the main subject of this sermon. None of us marvels that we neither recognize nor acknowledge the acts of God by reason alone, because we know that these acts can only be discerned spiritually. But those in whose hearts the grace of God shines, who are taught by God Himself – why are they so weak in faith? Why is their assent to God's law so limited, so mingled with fear and wavering? It seems strange that they should ever think that God's law would fail them. But if we stop and think about it, such weakness of faith will not seem strange to us.

When we consider the things we believe to be true in and of themselves, it may be said that faith is more certain than science. Even that which we know either by our senses or by the most infallible scientific demonstration is not as certain to us as the principal conclusions of Christian faith when they are grounded in what I will call the 'certainty of evidence' or the 'certainty of adherence'.

What I mean by the 'certainty of evidence' occurs when the mind assents to a proposition not because it is true in itself, but because its truth is evident or manifest to our reason. Even if something is in itself true, that will not persuade us unless its truth is made clearly evident to us. Thus, although it is as certain that there are spirits as that there are men, we are more inclined to believe in the existence of men than of spirits because they are so evident to our senses. Some propositions are so evident to our minds that no one who hears them affirmed can doubt their truth – such as, 'a part of anything is less than the whole'.

If this kind of certainty applied to matters of faith, then, since all people are equal in this regard, no one would be more certain or more doubtful than another. But in matters of faith, we find the contrary situation. Angels and spirits of the righteous in heaven have certainty about things spiritual because they have their evidence by the light of divine glory. On the other hand, that which we here on earth see only by the light of grace is not so certain as that which we see by sensory evidence or human reason.

Proofs are vain and frivolous unless they are more certain than what they seek to prove. Do we not see everywhere in Scripture how the Spirit tries to prove matters of belief by confirming them with rational arguments that will appeal to our senses? I conclude, therefore, that we have less 'certainty of evidence' about things taken on faith than about things perceived by the senses or grasped by our reason. And yet, who among us does not have doubts at some time or another about even this sort of evidence? I will not here recount the confessions of the most perfect of persons who ever lived on earth concerning their doubts. If I did so, I would only belabour a matter well known to every honest person of faith.

By the 'certainty of adherence', I mean that inclination of the heart to stick fast to what it believes. This is a greater certainty for us than what we believe through reason because as Christians we know that God's laws and promises are not only true, they are also good. Therefore, even when evidence of the truth of God's promises is so small that a man must grieve for the weakness of his faith in them, he still feels an adherence to them in his heart because he has at some time tasted the heavenly sweetness and the goodness of those promises. So he will strive against all reason to hope against hope that God's promises are true. With Job, he holds to the immovable resolution: although God shall kill him, he will never stop trusting Him. Why? Not so much because God's law is true, but because it is forever imprinted on his heart that it is *good* for him to remain faithful to God.

To be sure, our minds are so darkened with the foggy damp of original corruption that none of us has a heart so enlightened in knowledge or so firm in love of God's promise of salvation that his faith is perfect and free of doubt. If there were any such persons, they would be justified by their own inherent righteousness. Then what need would there be for the righteousness of Christ? His garment would be superfluous. If this were the case, we would be honourably clothed with our own robes of righteousness. But let that one beware who claims a spiritual power he has not, lest he lose the comfort of the weakness he does have!

One might try to show, although without good grounds, that it is possible to have perfect certainty in matters of faith. It has been asserted that Abraham never doubted. It has also been claimed that God gave us a special spirit that emboldens us to call Him Father and to open our eyes so that the truth of what we believe by faith will be evident to our minds. This spirit, we are told, is mightier than the light of the natural reason by which we discern sensible things. If this were true, we would need to be much more certain of what we believe than we are of what we see with our eyes, more certain of the grace of God in Jesus Christ than we are of the light of the sun that shines upon our faces.

To the argument that Abraham did not doubt, I reply that Scripture does not say he never doubted, but only that he did not doubt because of lack of faith in God. His was not the doubt of the unbeliever. His was the doubt of the ordinary believing man whose faith is weak. That Abraham was not void of all doubting what greater proof do we need than the evidence of his own words in the 17th verse of the 17th chapter of Genesis? There he doubts God's promise that his wife Sarah can bear a child at such an advanced age.[4]

As for the claim that the spirit of God within us gives us certain evidence, free of doubt, of His truth, this would be so if God had chosen to work like the natural agents made evident to us by their effects, such as fire which inflames our senses or sun which lightens our natural world. But in His incomprehensible wisdom, God has decided to limit the visible effects of His power to that degree which seems best to Him. Therefore He provides us with certainty in all that we need to know for salvation in the life to come. But He does not give us certain knowledge to achieve perfection in this life.

Even so, O God, it has pleased You, and so it is best for us that because we feel our own doubt and infirmity, we can no more breathe than we must pray: Dear God, help the infirmity of our belief.

I trust that now I have said enough to make clear my position on the question of the relation between evidence and faith.

— *Belief* —

Now I turn to the fourth and principal question raised by our text: namely, whether by the mere thought that God had failed him, the prophet Habakkuk drowned God's spirit within himself, fell from faith, and showed himself to be an unbeliever. This question is momentous. The peace and tranquillity of all souls depends on the answer. However we cast our response for Habakkuk, it will be the same for all of us.

In so far as the matter at hand is precious and dear to us, it behoves us to wade into it with great care, taking special heed for what we construct and to make sure that the foundation we build on is not mere stubble. If the doctrine we teach here is full of comfort and consolation, the basis for it must be sound. Otherwise, we will not save but deceive both ourselves and others.

I know that I am not deceived and that I cannot deceive you when I teach the truth that the faith whereby you are saved cannot fail you. It did not fail Habakkuk. It will not fail you.

In order to demonstrate this truth, I need to show the difference between Habakkuk's doubt and that of unbelievers, in this and other weaknesses of faith. There was in Habakkuk what St John calls the 'seed of God' which is planted in the hearts of all who are incorporated into Christ.[5] But this does not mean that we will never sin. Nor does it mean that we will never doubt God's promises. If we think that, we deceive ourselves. What God's grace, poured into His people, assures us is that, despite all sin and all doubt, we will never be separated from His love or cut off from Christ Jesus. The seed of God abides for ever in His children and shields them from receiving any irremediable wound.

When the faith of a child of God is at its strongest, it is still weak; but even at its weakest, that faith is so strong that it will never completely fail – never perish – even in those who think it is extinguished within them.

I know that there are those who will not be readily convinced or comforted by my argument because, like Habakkuk, they are suffering such agonies of grief over their apparently lost faith that their judgement is confounded and they cannot find their true selves within themselves. They search diligently for what lies all the while within their hearts and lament for a thing that seems past finding. They mourn like Rachel and refuse to be comforted, acting as if that which does exist does not, as if they did not believe in God when they do, as if they despaired, when in fact they do not.

In some grieving persons I grant that what we have is a melancholy spirit that comes from some physical infirmity, which can often be dispelled by healing the body. But there are three other reasons why people become so deeply depressed that they seem to lose their faith. One of these is a despair that comes from deciding that their faith has failed because others seem to have fared better in life or that they themselves were better off at some other stage in their lives.

A second reason for despair over apparent loss of faith is the false idea that people of faith will be joyful and happy. Since I am not, therefore I must have lost my faith. It is true that St Paul prayed for the church at Rome that 'the God of hope fill you with all joy of believing'.[6] But he did not mean by this that when we have a 'heaviness of spirit' and fail to find a singing joy and delight in our hearts, we have lost faith.

This joy, this light, is but a separable accident of faith and not a proof of faith. We would not even know such delight if we did not also experience a healthy intercourse with the darkness of despair. Too much honey turns to gall, and too much joy, even spiritual joy, will make us immoral, malicious, wilful. Happier by far is that person whose soul is humbled with inner desolation than he whose heart is puffed up and exalted beyond all reason by an abundance of spiritual delight. Better sometimes to go down into the pit with one who, beholding the darkness and bewailing the loss of inner joy and consolation, says from the bottom of lowest hell, 'My God, my God, why have You forsaken me?' than continually to walk arm and arm with angels; to sit, as it were, in the bosom of Abraham and to have no doubt and no thought except, 'I thank God it is not with me as with other men.'

No! Our God will have those who are to walk in His light feel from time to time what it is to sit in the shadow of death. A grieving spirit is, therefore, no argument for a faithless mind.

A third reason why some wrongly judge themselves to be without faith is that they base their judgement in such matters on the unreliable conclusions of their own limited rational capacities. Such persons proclaim that their unbelief has full dominion over them – possesses them. 'If I were faithful,' they say, 'it would not be thus with me.' They ignore the promptings of the spirit of faith which are groaning within them, heard by God even though they themselves hear nothing. There is no doubt that our faith can operate secretly within us, unknown to us, yet known to God.

But we will have little success convincing a person who has too hard an opinion of himself that he is not as weak in faith as he feels himself to be. He will tell you that he has thoroughly considered and exquisitely sifted all the corners of his heart and sees all there is within him and knows that he no longer believes in God.

Well, for sake of argument, let us grant what such people imagine – that they are indeed faithless and without belief. Are they not grieved by their unbelief? They are. Do they not wish for and even strive to regain their lost faith? We know that they do.

But where does this striving for what is lost come from? It comes from a secret love that they have for the object of their lost belief. No one can love what he believes to be non-existent. And without faith no person accepts the existence of what is believed. This argument cannot be dissolved by all the subtleties of the devil. Hence man's grief for what he has lost is a certain proof that he has not lost it.

The faith of true believers, therefore, although it may suffer many great and grievous downfalls, continues invincible. Faith conquers doubt and restores itself in the end. The dangerous conflicts to which it is subjected are not able to prevail against it. The prophet Habakkuk remained faithful despite the weakness of his faith.

— *Doubt* —

How true it is of our weak and wavering nature that we have no sooner received a grace than we are ready to fall from it; we have no sooner given our assent to the unfailing sanction of law than our very next notion is that the law is failing us. Although we find in ourselves a most willing heart to embrace God, even so far as to affirm unfeignedly with Peter, 'Lord, I am ready to go with you into prison and death,' yet how soon and how easily and with what small provocation we fall away when we are left to ourselves. The Galatians were content to pluck out their own eyes on one day for the sake of those who taught them the truth of Christ. The very next day they would pluck out the eyes of these very same teachers. The love they felt for Paul, the Angel of Ephesus, how greatly inflamed, and then how quickly extinguished!

The higher we flow, the nearer we are to an ebb, when we are seen as mere men driven in the course of our own inclination without the heavenly support of the Holy Spirit.

Again, the desire of our spiritual enemies is so incredible and their means to overthrow our faith so strong that those whom the blessed Apostle knew were betrothed and made fast to Christ, even to them he wrote with great trembling: 'I am jealous over you with a godly jealousy because I have prepared for you one husband, to present you a pure virgin to Christ. But I fear lest, as the serpent beguiled Eve through his subtlety, so your minds will be corrupted from the simplicity that is in Christ.'[7]

The simplicity of faith takes the naked promise of God – His bare word – and on that alone it rests. This simplicity the Serpent labours continually to pervert, corrupting the mind with vain imaginings of repugnancy and contrariness between the promise of God and those things which our senses and our experiences or some other knowledge have made obvious to us. The word of God's promise to His people is: 'I will not leave nor forsake you.' Upon this the simplicity of faith rests and is not afraid.[8]

But mark how Satan subtly corrupts the minds of that 'rebellious generation whose spirits do not remain faithful to God'. They beheld the desolate state of the desert they were in and by the supposed wisdom of their senses concluded that God's promise was but folly. Can God prepare a table in this wilderness? The word of promise to Sarah was: 'Thou shalt bear a son.' Faith is simple and does not doubt. But Satan corrupts this simplicity and entangles the mind of the woman with an argument from common experience: a woman who is old – how can she be acquainted again with the passions of youth?[9]

God's promise to Moses and the prophets made the Saviour of the world so apparent to Philip that in his simplicity he could conceive of no other messiah than Jesus, the son of Joseph. But, to keep Nathaniel from seeing and being saved, Satan cast a mist before his eyes, putting into his head the common notion about Nazareth that it is not possible that a good thing could come from that place.[10]

This strategy Satan uses with such great dexterity that people are bereft of all perseverance in the faith that could relieve them and give them comfort. Yes, he even takes from them all remembrance of things with which they are most familiar. Surely, the people of Israel could not forget that the God who had led them across the sea would be able and willing to feed them in the desert. But this knowledge was obliterated by the awareness of their present needs. They felt God's hand against them in the food they ate and forgot that it was His hand that had delivered them from their oppressor.

Sarah was not at that time to know that with God all things were possible. Nathaniel failed to remember that God chooses base things of this world to disgrace those that are most highly esteemed by us. The prophet Habakkuk knew that the promise of God's grace, protection and favour to His people did not grant immunity from punishment for their misdoings. He knew that even as God has said, 'My mercies I will continue for ever towards them,' He has also said, 'their transgressions I will punish with a rod.'[11] He knew that it is unreasonable that we should set the measure of our own punishment and tell God how great or how long our sufferings should be. He knew that we are blind to and altogether ignorant of what is truly best for us. He knew that we often act unwisely against our own interests, asking for a serpent when, in fact, we crave a fish. He knew that, although what we ask for may be good, God often defers our petitions so that we may learn to desire great things greatly. All this he knew.

Yet beholding the land that God had set aside for His own people and seeing it occupied by heathen nations, and seeing how they ruined the land and made waste of it for their own wicked pleasures, and beholding the Lord's own throne made into a heap of stones and His Temple defiled with the carcasses of his servants cast out for the birds of the air to devour and the flesh of innocent ones thrown out for the beasts of the field to feed upon, Habakkuk remembered how long and how earnestly he had cried to God to help His people for the sake of His Name as well as for their sakes. The repugnancy of the discrepancy between the horror that filled his senses and his faith in the promise of God's law made such a deep impression on him that he did not examine the problem carefully. He simply inferred that 'the law of God has failed'.

Which of us here cannot soberly advise his brother, 'Sir, you must learn to strengthen your faith by what your own past experience has shown you of God's great goodness toward you. Do you not acknowledge that you have received much? Let that be the proof that you will receive more. When you doubt what you shall have in the future, remember what at God's hands you have had in the past. Make this reckoning: the benefits He has bestowed thus far are our vouchers, our guarantees, for what will come to us in the future. His present mercy is a warrant for His future love, because those whom He loves He loves to the end.'

Although God's goodness to us in reconciling love is so great that we cannot measure it by the number of hours, days, and years of our lives, if we put all these acts together they lack the force to overcome the doubt that comes from the fear of losing a tiny transitory favour from our fellows, or some small calamity. We immediately imagine that we are crossed clean out of God's book, that He favours others, does not love us and passes us by like a stranger who no longer knows us.

Then, as we look at other people and compare them to ourselves, we conclude that their tables are richly furnished every day whereas ashes and dirt are our daily bread; they sing happily before the beautiful music of the lute and their children dance for them, whereas our hearts are as heavy as lead, our sighs are thick and our pulses too fast, our tears wash the beds in which we lie. The sun shines fair on them whereas we are hung up like wineskins blackened in the smoke, cast into corners like chards of a broken pot. Do not tell us about the promises of God! Tell those who reap the fruit of God's love. The promises of God belong not to us but to others. God, forgive our weakness, but this is the way it is with us.

— *The Certainty of Faith* —

Well, let the frailty of our nature, the subtlety of Satan, the force of our own deceivable imaginations all be as we know them to be – ready at every moment to threaten the utter subversion of our faith. Yet, faith is never really at risk.

Our Father, the prophets, and our Lord and Master have often spoken it and by long experience we have found it to be true that no one's condition is as sure as ours. The prayer of Christ on our behalf is more than sufficient to strengthen us be we ever so weak, and to overthrow any power threatening us be it ever so strong and potent.

Christ's prayer for us does not preclude the need for action on our part. Their thoughts are vain who think that they can preserve a city that God Himself is not willing to save. Is it not just as vain of them to think that God will save a city if the inhabitants are not careful to watch over it themselves? The husbandman may not therefore burn his plough nor the merchant forsake his trade merely because God has promised, 'I will not fail you.' God's promise does not make it an indifferent matter whether we act rightly or not, whether we attend to reading of His Word or not, whether we pray to be saved from temptation or not. Surely, if we intend to stand in the faith of the Son of God we must continue hourly to strive to provide for ourselves. When our Lord and Saviour said, 'Father, keep them in Thy Name,' He never meant that we should be careless about taking care of ourselves. [12]

The earth may shake, the pillars of the world may tremble under us, the countenance of heaven may be overshadowed, and the sun may lose his light, the moon her beauty, the stars their glory. But concerning the man who trusts in God, if the fire cannot singe a hair on his head, if lions and other beasts driven by ravenous hunger to devour his flesh instead adore this faithful man, then who is there in this whole world who can overthrow his faith or alter his affection toward God or God's affection for him?

If I remember this, who can separate me from my God? 'Shall tribulation or anguish or persecution or famine or nakedness or peril or sword? No. I am persuaded that neither tribulation nor anguish nor persecution nor famine nor nakedness nor peril nor sword nor death nor life nor angels nor principalities nor powers nor things present nor things to come nor height nor depth nor any other creature' shall ever prevail over me. [13]

I know in whom I have faith. I am not ignorant of whose precious blood has been shed for me. I have a shepherd who is full of kindness, full of care, full of power. To Him I commit myself. His own finger has engraved this sentence on my heart: 'Satan has desired to winnow you as wheat, but I have prayed that your faith in me shall not fail.' [14] To the end of my days, therefore, I will labour to maintain the assurance of my faith, like a jewel. By a combination of my efforts and the gracious mediation of God's prayer I shall keep my faith.

Notes

1. In the spirit of this modern edition, I have taken the necessary liberty of providing new titles, subheadings and paragraphing (as did John Keble in his

nineteenth-century editions) for all of Hooker's sermons and tracts.

2. Thomas Fuller, *The History of the Worthies of England* (J.G.W.L., London, 1662), Vol. I, 264.
3. On the few occasions, as here, when I have substituted a modern edition of the Bible for Hooker's *Geneva Bible*, I have used *The New English Bible* and so indicated with the designation NEB.
4. 'Abraham threw himself down on his face; he laughed and said to himself: "Can a son be born to a man who is a hundred years old? Can Sarah bear a son when she is ninety?"' (NEB)
5. 1 John 3.9: 'A child of God does not commit sin, because the divine seed remains in him.' (NEB)
6. Romans 15.13.
7. 2 Corinthians 11.2–3.
8. Joshua 1.5; Hebrews 13.5.
9. Psalms 78.19; Genesis 18.12.
10. John 1.45–46.
11. Psalms 89.28, 32.
12. Deuteronomy 31.6; John 17.11.
13. Romans 8.35, 38, 39.
14. Luke 22.31–32.

— 2 —
Threats to the Faith

This sermon, known traditionally as 'The First Sermon on Jude', is one of two published by Joseph Barnes in 1614 under the title, 'Two Sermons on S. Judes Epistle'. The Jude sermons are the earliest extant writings we have from Hooker, probably dating from 1582 or 1583, shortly before he began his tenure as Master of the Temple Church. He may have preached them while serving as rector at Drayton Beauchamp parish, or, perhaps, he delivered them in the chapel at Corpus Christi College, Oxford.

The theme here is consistent with Hooker's later writings in which he warns against the threats to Christian faith from false beliefs and false prophets, whether they come from Rome or Geneva. It is not surprising that Hooker found St Jude a congenial spirit in his own struggle against what he saw as the great danger to church unity and to the faith of English Christians from Puritan radicals and Roman Catholic recusants. The tone is clearly more anti-Catholic than his later writings, which tended to have a more anti-Puritan flavour. [1]

In a broader sense, these two sermons on Jude are part of Hooker's ongoing analysis of Christian faith.

> ***But you, my friends, should remember the predictions made by the apostles of our Lord Jesus Christ. This was the warning they gave you: 'In the final age there will be men who pour scorn on religion, and follow their own godless lusts.' These men draw a line between spiritual and unspiritual persons, although they are themselves wholly unspiritual. But you, my friends, must fortify yourselves in your most sacred faith. Continue to pray in the power of the Holy Spirit. Keep yourselves in the love of God, and look forward to the day when our Lord Jesus Christ in his mercy will give eternal life.*** Jude 17–21 (NEB)

— *Enemies Within the Church* —

Both the occasion and the purpose of St Jude are clearly opened to our understanding at the outset and throughout the entire Epistle. There were then, as there are now, many evil and wickedly disposed persons who, although not of the mystical body of the Church, are within her visible bounds. They are persons who are predestined to condemnation, ungodly people who turn God's grace into licence to sin and deny the Lord Jesus. The spirit of the Lord moves through the hand of Jude (the servant of Jesus and brother of James) to exhort those who are called and sanctified by God the Father earnestly to maintain the faith which was once delivered to the Saints.[2]

This faith we cannot maintain unless we know perfectly, first, who the enemy is, and second, how to keep the faith. The first three verses in the scripture I have just read describe plainly who are the enemies of the cross of Christ, and the second two verses give a sweet lesson to those who love the Lord Jesus about how to establish and strengthen their faith.

Let us first examine the description of these faithless reprobates and then come to the words of the exhortation which teaches Christians how to rest their hearts on God's eternal and everlasting truth. The description of these godless persons is twofold: general and particular. The general description identifies what sort of men they are; the particular points directly at them and names them. In the general description of them, we have to consider these things: first, when were they identified? 'They were told of before'; secondly, who identified them? 'They were spoken of by the Apostles of our Lord Jesus Christ'; thirdly, when would they be exposed to the world? 'In the last time'; fourthly, what is their disposition and demeanour? They are 'mockers and walkers after their own ungodly lusts'.[3]

In the third chapter of his letter to the Philippians, the Apostle Paul describes with certainty that 'They are men of whom I have told you often, and now with tears I tell you of them again. Their God is their belly; their glorying and rejoicing is their shame; they attend only to earthly things.'[4]

These then were the enemies of the cross of Christ whom Paul saw. His eyes gushed forth tears when he beheld them. But we are told how the Apostles also spoke of enemies whom they had not yet seen, a family of men as yet unheard of, a generation reserved for the end of the world, for the last days. These Apostles not only declared what they had heard and seen in their own time, but also prophesied about men in times to come. 'You do well,' said St Peter, 'if you take heed to the words of prophecy so that you understand this: no prophecy in the Scripture comes from men.'[5] All prophecy in Scripture comes from the secret inspiration of God.

— *False Prophets and True Prophets* —

But there are other prophecies which are not based on Scripture. Indeed, there are prophecies that are contrary to Scripture. Pay attention to prophecies but only to those that are in Scripture. Both the style and the content of these show us that they are from God. As to the question of how men of Spirit prophesied in Holy Scripture, we must understand that their knowledge and how they uttered it came not by the usual means by which we are given some grasp of the mysteries of our salvation or the usual means we use to instruct others in such matters. Everything we know comes from the hands and the ministrations of men, who lead us along like children from letter to syllable to word to line to sentence to paragraph to page. But God Himself was the instructor of the true prophets. He taught them, partly by dreams and visions in the night, partly by revelations in the daylight, taking them aside and talking with them as one might with his neighbour. Those who receive such inspiration are acquainted with the secret and hidden counsels of God. They see things that they themselves are unable to describe – things that astonish both men and angels. They are given to understand what is going to happen in the last days.

Thus God, who has lighted the eyes of the prophets' understanding by such unusual and extraordinary means, now performs another miracle. He Himself frames and fashions the very words and writings of the prophets so that there seems to be no difference between their manner of speech and ours.

Whenever we conceive a thing in our hearts and thoroughly understand it within ourselves, how great, how long, how earnest is the meditation we are forced to use before we can utter it in such a way that our brothers and sisters might receive some instruction and comfort from our mouths. After much travail and much pain, when we finally open our lips to speak of the wonderful works of God, our tongues falter within our mouths. Many times we disgrace the dreadful mysteries of our faith and grieve the spirit of our listeners with unsavoury words and unseemly speeches.

Yet behold how even the worst among us, compared with the prophets, seem to talk of God as babes in arms might speak of weighty matters of state. Those whose words show forth wisdom, whose lips utter the purest knowledge, so long as they comprehend and speak as human beings, do they not in various ways have to make excuses for themselves? Sometimes they wisely acknowledge, in the words of the Book of Wisdom, 'Scarcely can we discern things happening here on earth and only with great labour do we find out things that are in the future. Who then can discover what is in heaven?'[6]

Sometimes our wisest men confess with Job that they are seeking things too 'wonderful for us' and have 'spoken we know not what'.[7] Sometimes they end their discourses like the Book of Maccabees: 'If we have done well, as the course requires, that is all we desire. If we have spoken sparingly, we have done all that we could do.'[8]

But Isaiah says, 'God has made my mouth like a sword.'[9] And the Apostle Paul says, 'Not the spirit of this world but the Spirit of God gives us knowledge of the things of God, which we speak about not in the words which man's wisdom teaches but in words taught by the Holy Spirit.'[10] This is what the prophets meant when they spoke of 'books written fully from within and without'. These were the books given to them as food to be eaten.[11]

With the true prophets, it is God, through the Holy Spirit, who forms the very words which are spoken to us. This is not to say that

God literally fed the prophets with ink and paper, but that when God was using them for His heavenly work, He assumed that they never spoke or wrote any word of their own, but uttered syllable for syllable as He put it into their mouths. They were as mute as a harp or a lute until used at the discretion of a skilled musician. Unlike the harp or lute, which are inanimate, unfeeling, and have no self-understanding, the prophets and holy men of God felt the power of their own words. When they spoke of our peace, every corner of their hearts was filled with joy. When they prophesied of the mournings, lamentations and woes that would fall upon us, they wept in the bitterness and indignation of the spirit, the arm of the Lord being mighty and strong upon them.

All prophecies based on Holy Scripture are formed in this same manner. But, as one star differs from another in its glory, so every word of prophecy has its own treasure of truth in it. All are not of equal importance, just as all treasures are not of equal value. The chief and principal truth of prophesying is the promise of righteousness, peace, holiness, glory, victory, immortality for every soul that believes that Jesus is the Christ, the Jew first, and then the Gentile.

This central prophecy calls us to believe the improbable truth that our salvation comes through a man who seemed outwardly to be forsaken of God, judged and condemned with the wicked, buffeted on the face, scoffed at by soldiers, scourged by tormentors, hanged on a cross, pierced to the heart, and heard by many witnesses to roar, in the anguish of His soul, as if His heart had been rent asunder, 'Oh, my God, why hast Thou forsaken me?'

I say to you that such a doctrine of salvation seems so improbable to a natural person that whether we preach it to the Gentile or to the Jew, the one will condemn our faith as madness, the other as blasphemy. In order to strengthen our faith in this central prophecy and to confirm the certainty of the saving truth in the hearts of men, the Lord mingled with the preachings that He sent immediately to reveal these things, prophecies of other events both civil and religious that were to come to pass in every age until the last of the latter days. He did this so that, as we saw these various prophecies fulfilled, we would have consolation in the hope of things not yet seen. For as one thing was accomplished and then another, and a third, we would see plainly that God is leading us along by the hand until He settles us upon the rock of an assured hope that all will be fulfilled. Thus it was not in vain for Jude to prophesy concerning those godless wicked ones 'who were spoken of before'.

Now, we must ask, who are those who may rightly condemn the wicked among us? The answer is he who truly loves Jesus – and woe to him who does not! Such a person is known by the fact that he loves and follows Jesus' Apostles. He does not despise the behaviour and words of the Apostles. He does not despise their poverty and simplicity. Worldly and carnal men wrongly honour and dishonour, credit and discredit the words and deeds of others according to what they lack. If a rich and well-attired man comes among us, though he be a thief or murderer, or whatever the condition of his heart, so long as his coat is purple or velvet or silk, everyone rises up and all of our reverent solemnities are never sufficient. Even among us, a person who truly serves God will be condemned and despised if he is poor.

But has not God chosen the refuse of the world, the outcasts of society, to be the lights of the world? And what of the very Apostles of Christ? Here are men unlearned, yet how filled with understanding; few in number, yet how great in power; contemptible in appearance, yet how clothed in the Spirit. How wonderful they are!

If I wish to gain true understanding, whom shall I seek to teach me? Shall I get me to the schools of the Greeks? Why? These men of worldly wisdom are dumb because they have rejected the wisdom of God. Shall I beseech the scribes and interpreters of the law to be my teachers? How can they be wise when they are offended by the cross of Christ? I must have a true teacher because it is death for me to be ignorant of the great mystery of the Son of God. Yet I would have been ignorant for ever were it not for one of these Apostles of Jesus, a poor fisherman, unknown, unlearned, recently emerging from his boat with clothes wringing wet, who opened his inspired mouth and taught me: 'In the beginning was the Word, and the Word was with God, and the Word was God.' These Apostles, these poor simple folk, have made us rich in the knowledge of the mysteries of Christ.

Remember, therefore, what the Apostles speak about. If the children of this world do not regard the words of the Apostles, is it any wonder? The Apostles are the followers of the Lord, not of anyone born of this world. It is true that a person sworn to this world is not capable of grasping that faith which the Apostles teach. Why then, do such people frequent the courts of our God? You who are children of this world have your own lord who has provided you with your own apostles and teachers: Chaldeans, wizards, soothsayers, astrologers, and such like.[12] Listen to them. Tell us not that you will sacrifice to our God if we will sacrifice to yours, and that if we will read your scriptures and listen to your traditions and if you may have Mass with us, then we may have communion with you, and that you will admit the things spoken of by the Apostles our Lord Jesus, if your lord and master can have his ordinances observed and his statutes kept by us.

Solomon took it as evident proof that a woman cannot have a motherly affection for her child if she agrees to have it cut into parts. You cannot love the Lord Jesus with all your heart if you lend one ear to His Apostles and another to false apostles. This carries us to a mingle-mangle of religion and superstition. Ministers and priests, light and darkness, truth and error, traditions and Scripture. No. We have no Lord but Jesus, no doctrine but the Gospel, no teachers but His Apostles.[13]

Is it reasonable to require English subjects to obey the laws and edicts of Spain? I simply marvel that anyone bearing the name of 'servant of Jesus Christ' will go about trying to draw us from our allegiance. We are His sworn subjects. It is not lawful for us to heed things which are not told to us by His Apostles. The Apostles have told us that in the last days there will be 'mockers' of our faith. Therefore, we believe that will be so. *Credimus quia legimus*. (We believe what we read.) If we did not read something in Scripture, we would not teach it.

— *Mockers and Atheists* —

The third item we agreed to consider in our description of these mockers of our faith is the matter of when they are to appear. We are told that it will happen in 'the last time'. We may suppose that Jude meant to note a special calamity peculiar to each of the ages and generations yet to come. In each generation, the Church is a mixture of true believers and wicked mockers. Noah, at the commandment of God, built an ark and there were in it beasts of all sorts, clean and unclean. A husbandman plants a vineyard and looks for grapes, but when he comes to the harvest, he finds wild and sour grapes together with the sweet grapes. A rich man 'prepares a great supper and invites many', but when he sits down, he finds here and there strangers seated among his friends. This has been the state of the Church since the beginning. God has always mingled his Saints with faithless and godless persons – as it were, the clean with the unclean, good grapes with sour, friends and children with aliens and strangers.

Marvel not, then, if in the last days you see people with whom you live and walk arm-in-arm laughing at your religion and blaspheming that glorious Name to whom you are called. Thus it was in the days of the patriarchs and prophets. Are we better than they are?

The fourth point I wish to consider is the characteristics of these mockers, these worst of men. These are those who use religion as a cloak to put off and on as the weather requires; who hear the preaching of St John the Baptist today, and tomorrow agree to Herod's decision to have him beheaded; who worship Christ while all the time planning some massacre in their hearts; who kiss Christ, with Judas, and then betray Christ, with Judas. These are the mockers.

As Ishmael, the son of Hagar, laughed at Isaac who was the heir to God's promise to Israel, so shall these mockers laugh at you as the maddest people under the sun, if you, like Moses, choose to suffer affliction with the people of God, rather than enjoy the pleasures of sin for a season. And why do they mock you so?

Because, unlike you, God has not given them the eyes to see nor the hearts to conceive the abundant rewards awaiting you in the promise of salvation. Such promises can bring them no pleasure, just as Ishmael could take no pleasure in God's promise to Abraham that Isaac would be his heir, because that promise did not apply to him but to Isaac.[14]

These men are called 'mockers' because of their impiety to God. For the impurity of their language and their tongues they are called 'walkers after their own ungodly lusts'.[15]

St Peter, in the third chapter of his second epistle, sounds the very depth of the impiety of these mockers, showing first how they have no shame in openly professing their blasphemy by flatly denying the Gospel of Jesus Christ and by deriding the sweet and comfortable promises of His appearing to us. Peter also tells us how these mockers among us dispute God by using truth to subvert truth, even Scripture to disprove Scripture.

As atheists, the mockers cannot help but be beasts in conversation. Why do they remove themselves from God's love in this way? Why do they take pains to abandon and put out of their hearts all taste, all feeling of religion? They do so because only thus can they give themselves over to lust and unclean behaviour without feelings of inner remorse or guilt. Being mockers of God, these people are of necessity followers of their own ungodly lusts.

Surely, the state of these persons is more lamentable than is the condition of pagans or Turks or Jews. At the bare beholding of heaven and earth, the infidel's heart quickly showed him glimpses of an eternal, an infinite, immortal, and everliving God, whose hands had fashioned and framed the world. The light of natural reason put some wisdom and understanding in the mind and heart of the pagans. Bring such a pagan to the schools of the prophets, rebuke him, lay the judgements of God upon him, show him the sins of his inner heart, and he will fall down and worship God.

Even those who crucified the Lord were not so far past recovery that the preaching of the Apostles failed to have some influence on them. Although the Jews, for lack of correct knowledge, have not submitted themselves to the righteousness of God, they have, as Paul says in Romans, a certain religious zeal. Even secular Athenian humanists, possessing neither religious zeal nor correct knowledge, have some religion in them. But these mockers, walking after their own ungodly lusts, have smothered every spark of heavenly light and stifled even their God-given natural understanding.[16] Oh, Lord God! Your mercy is over all Your works. You save man and beast. Yet a happy thing it would be for these people if they had never been born. And so, I leave them.

St Jude, his mind being well trained in the doctrines of the Apostles concerning what was to happen at the end of time, was a wise man of sound judgement. He was grieved to see many falling away from the faith that they had previously professed. I say that he was grieved, not that he was dismayed. He could see in the faces of some a change that showed they were half in doubt about whether they had deceived themselves in believing the Gospel of Jesus Christ. St Jude tried to comfort and refresh these simple lambs by taking them up in his arms and showing them those men who were causing great offence. Look at the true cause of your weakening faith. Look at those who have forsaken the blessed faith in which you still stand. They are right before your eyes. Look at them closely. Mark them. Are they not carnal? Are they not like filthy carrion cast out in the dirt? Is there that spirit in them which leads you to call on the name of God your Father, Abba? Why should you be discomforted by them? Have you not heard from the Apostles that there would be such mockers in the last time? These verily are they that now separate themselves from us.

— *True Believers Judge Not* —

So that you may better see what all this division and separation among members of the Church means, we must understand that the great multitude of true believers, however dispersed they may be from one another, are all of one body of which Christ is the head, one building, of which He is the cornerstone. As members of this body, they are knit together. As stones of the building they are coupled and used to become the temple of the Lord. They grow into men of perfect stature. That which links Christ to us is His mercy and love toward us. That which ties us to Him is our faith in the promised salvation revealed to us in the Word of truth. That which unites and joins us to one another as though we were of one heart and soul is our love.

Those who are inwardly in their hearts lively members of this body and polished stones of this building, coupled and joined to Christ as flesh of His flesh and bone of His bone, are linked and fastened to each other by the mutual bond of His unspeakable love towards them, their uncontrived faith in Him and their sincere and hearty affection for one another. No one can tell, of course, who is a true believer and who is, inwardly, an unbelieving Jew; no one can tell except God whose eyes alone behold the secret disposition of all men's hearts.

We whose eyes are too dim to behold the inner person must leave the judgement of each to the Lord, taking everyone as he presents himself and accounting all as brothers and sisters, assuming that Christ loves them tenderly so long as they continue to profess the Gospel and to join outwardly in the communion of Saints. At any time that they outwardly fall away from and forsake either the Gospel or their church membership, then there is no harm in calling them what they are: *autokatakpitoi* (self-condemned).[17] When they separate themselves from us, they are judged not by us but by their own actions.

— *Schism, Heresy and Apostasy* —

People separate themselves from the Church in several ways: heresy, schism, apostasy. If they loose the ties of faith by openly opposing any principal point of Christian doctrine, they have separated themselves by heresy. If they break the bonds of unity which hold together the body of the Church by wilfully forsaking the holy, pure and orderly exercises established in the Church, they have separated themselves by schism. If they wilfully cast off and forsake both profession of Christ and communion with Christians and take leave of all religion, they have separated themselves by apostasy.

It was not the pressure of others that forced apostates to leave the Church; it was not any infirmity or weakness in them; it was not fear of persecution; it was not grief over punishments they suffered and could no longer endure. No. They voluntarily separated themselves from the Church with a fully conceived and determined intention never again to call on the name of Jesus or to have any fellowship with his Saints. Because the hearts of infidels were hardened against the truth and the minds of our weaker brethren are much too disturbed by these bad examples, the Holy Ghost has pronounced judgement against these backsliders, declaring them to be worldly men without the spirit of Christ. This was so that no one need be overly amazed at or offended by the fall of such men. Otherwise, ordinary people, not seeing the evil in these men, might say to themselves: 'If Christ is the Son of the living God, if He gives the word of eternal life, if He is able to bring salvation to all who come to Him, what then is the meaning of this wilful departing from Him, this apostasy? Why would any of his servants ever forsake Him?'

Do not be deceived, my children. His true servants have not forsaken Him.

Those who separate themselves from Christ once lived among his servants; but if they truly had been his servants they never would have left Him. They lived among us, as St John says, but they were not of us. And St Jude proves this by noticing that their behaviour showed them to be carnal and not spiritual in nature. Would you judge wheat by the chaff that the wind scatters from it? Do your children have no bread because the dogs have not tasted it? Are Christians to be deceived in their hope for salvation because non-Christians have denied the existence of these joys which are to come in the next life? So what if these evil ones seemed to be pillars and principal upholders of our faith! What is that to us? We already know that angels have fallen down from heaven. If these men had been truly of us, they would have stood more certain than the angels and never departed from their places. As it is, we should not marvel at their departure at all. Nor should we be weakened in our faith by their falling away. They never were truly one of us. They were people of the flesh who lacked the spirit. My children, you abide in this house for ever. Those who are cast out are only slaves. [18]

Each of you should examine yourself to be certain whether you are a bondsman or a free child of God. I have already told you that we must beware not to presume to sit as little gods in judgement upon others and, as our mere opinion or fancy leads us, rashly to determine if this man is sincere or that man a hypocrite. They themselves make it known by actually separating themselves from us. Who are you that you take it upon yourselves to judge another? Judge yourself! God has given us infallible evidence whereby we may at any time give true and righteous sentence upon ourselves. We cannot examine the hearts of others. We may, however, examine our own hearts.

In fact, it is as easy a matter for the spirit within you to tell you whom you belong to as it is for your eyes to tell you where you are sitting or standing. For, what does Scripture say? 'You who were in the past strangers and enemies because your minds were set on evil works, Christ has now reconciled in the body of his flesh, through his death, to make you holy, unblameable and without fault in his sight.' [19]

We know who we are if we can make this confession:

> I was in past times dead through my trespasses and sin. I walked after the prince of the air and followed the spirit that makes men disobedient. But God, who is rich in mercy, through his great love, even when I was dead, quickened me in Christ. (Colossians 3)
>
> I was once fierce, heady, proud, high-minded; but God has made me like a newly weaned child. I loved pleasures more than God. I followed greedily the joy of this present world. I esteemed him that erected a stage or theatre more than Solomon who built a temple to the Lord. The harp, viola, timbrell, pipe, male and female singers were at my parties, and

I rejoiced to see my children dance before me. Of every kind of vanity I said: 'Oh, how sweet you are to my soul.'

To me all these things are now crucified, and I to them. I now hate the pride of this life, the pomp of the world. Now I take as great a delight in your way, O Lord, as in all riches. I find more joy of heart in my Lord and Saviour than does the worldly minded person when his wheat crop and his supply of oil are in abundance. Now I taste nothing sweet but the bread that comes down from heaven and gives life to the world. Now my eyes see nothing but Jesus rising from the dead. Now my ears close out all sorts of melodies in order to hear the song of them that have obtained victory over the beast [the devil] and his image, and his mark and the number of his name [666], and who stand on the sea of glass, playing harps of God, singing songs of Moses, and the song of the Lamb, saying, 'Great and marvellous are your works, Lord God Almighty; just and true are your ways, O King of Saints.'[20]

Surely, if the spirit within us has thus brought us to a regeneration and a new life, and if we endeavour to frame our outward lives anew, then we may boldly say with Paul, in the tenth chapter of his letter to the Hebrews, 'We are not of them which withdrew ourselves to hell, but we are of those which follow faith and save our souls.' For they that fall away from the grace of God and separate themselves unto perdition are fleshly and worldly; they have not God's Holy Spirit. But unto you, because you are his sons, God has sent the Spirit of his Son, so that you might know that Christ has built you upon an unmoveable rock, that He has registered your names in the book of life, that He has bound himself in a sure and everlasting covenant to be your God and the God of your children after you.

— *Arrogance of the Papacy* —

Here I must advertise to all people who have certainty of God's holy love within their breasts, how unkindly and injuriously some of our own countrymen and brethren have dealt with us over the past 24 years.[21] They act as if we were the evildoers of whom St Jude speaks. They never cease charging us with either schism or heresy or outright apostasy, as though we were the ones who had separated ourselves from Christ, utterly forsaken God, quite renounced heaven, and trampled all truth and all religion under our feet. For the charge of apostasy, God Himself will plead our cause in that day when they shall answer us for these words, and not we them. To those who accuse us of schism and heresy, we have often given a reasonable and, I trust, in God's sight, an allowable answer. For what they call heresy is but the way we worship the God of our fathers, believing all that is written in the law and the prophets. That which they call schism, we know to be our reasonable service to God and our obedience to his voice.

You Jesuits and papists, listen to me. You ought to know that the Father has given all power to the Son and has made Him the only head of His Church. Of course, it is true that Christ is the mystical head of the invisible Church. But even as He has reserved the mystical administration of his invisible Church to Himself, so has He committed the government of his visible congregations to the sons of David. These sons are those whom the Holy Ghost has set over them, to lead them into their several pastures, one to this congregation, another to that one.

No Pope or papist under heaven will ever be able to prove that these Romish bishops had legitimate supremacy over *all* churches by any word that is in Scripture. Even the children in our streets laugh them to scorn when they use the phrase, 'Thou art Peter,' to prove their case. Yet this is the sole basis for the opinion held throughout the world that the Pope is the universal head of all churches. But Jesus never said that. All He said was, '*Tu es Petrus*. You are Peter.' The Pope has no more reason to draw the authority for his claim to have universal authority over the Church from this passage than Christ's disciples had to conclude from his words at the end of John's Gospel that the 'disciple whom Jesus loved' (John) would never die.[22]

Being unable to brook the words of Christ which forbid his

disciples from behaving like worldly princes, this son of perdition, this man of sin [the Pope] has risen up and rebelled against his Lord and to strengthen himself, crept into the houses of most of the noble families in his country, taken their children from infancy to be his Cardinals, fawned on the kings and princes of the earth, and, by a kind of spiritual blackmail, induced them to sell their lawful authority and jurisdiction for such titles as *Catholicus*, *Christianismus*, *Defensor fidei*, and the like. He has also sold pardons to entrap the ignorant and built seminaries to lure young men desirous of learning. This, my friends, is the rock upon which his church is built! Here is the man who has grown huge and strong like the cedars which are not shaken in the wind, all because our princes have been like children – too tender-hearted to resist him.

And so it has come to pass, as you see today, that this man of sin wars against us, not by foreign invasion but by bringing the first fruits of our own bodies, our children, to eat us up, so that the bowels of the child may be the mother's grave. He causes no small number of our brethren to forsake their native country and, with all disloyalty, cast off their allegiance to our own dread sovereign, the Queen, whom God, in his mercy, has set over them, and for whose safety they should think the dearest blood in their bodies well-spent.

If I should here uncover the cup of those deadly and ugly abominations with which this Pope has made the earth so drunk that it has reeled under us, I know your godly hearts would be loath to see them. For my part, I take no delight to rake in such filth. I would rather take a garment and cover them while my face is turned away. Lord, open their eyes and, if possible, cause them to see how wretched, miserable, poor, blind, and naked they are. Put it, Lord, in their hearts to seek white raiment to cover themselves, so that their filthy nakedness may no longer be visible.

Beloved in Christ, let us hourly and heartily bow down our knees and lift our hands to heaven, each in his own chamber, and also together openly in our churches to pray for these papists. Let us do this even though the Pope has laid solemn sentence of excommunication against our country, even though he and his scholars, whom he has stolen from our very midst, have falsely charged our gracious lady, the Queen, and the rest of us, with abolishing prayers within the realm, with allowing sacrilege in God's service, with being unfaithful to God by putting on our throne what he calls a strumpet in place of a so-called virtuous ruler,[23] with abandoning fasting, abhorring confession, disliking penance, with liking usury, and with finding no good in celibacy. According to these charges, all who are under our religious care are not only worse off than when we received them, but corrupted as well. I have not added one word or syllable to the charges which Master Bristow,[24] a man raised here among us and sworn to the same loyalties as we, has recently delivered.

I appeal now to the conscience of everyone who has been truly converted by us to say whether our preaching failed ever to raise his heart up to God; whether our exhortations never wrung a penitent tear from his heart; whether his soul never reaped any joy, any comfort, any consolation in Christ Jesus, by means of our Sacraments, our prayers, and psalms and thanksgivings; whether he was never made better by our ministry – but always worse.

O merciful God! If heaven and earth in this case do not witness with us and against them, let us be torn out from the land of the living! Let the earth on which we stand swallow us up quickly. But if we belong to the Lord our God, and have not forsaken Him, that is to say, if amongst us God's blessed Sacraments are duly administered and his Holy Word preached sincerely and daily, then have no doubt that God is our captain.

Notes

1. For authoritative commentary on the provenance of the Jude sermons see W. Speed Hill, gen. ed., *The Folger Library Edition of the Works of Richard Hooker* Vols I–V (The Belknap Press of Harvard University, Cambridge, MA and London, 1977–1990), V, 1–7.
2. Jude 1–4.
3. Jude 17–18.
4. Philippians 3.18–19.
5. 2 Peter 1.19–20.
6. Wisdom 9.16.

7. Job 15.2, 3.
8. 2 Maccabees 15.39.
9. Isaiah 49.2.
10. 1 Corinthians 2.12–13.
11. Ezekiel 3.2–3.
12. Daniel 4.7; 5.7.
13. 1 Kings 3.1–28. This is one of the places where Hooker's transition is unclear. Probably he means to use the famous example of Solomon's wisdom to demonstrate that we must avoid the confusion of conflicting advisers who surround us and refer only to Holy Scripture for the advice of Christ and His Apostles. The transition to the next paragraph is even more obscure. Hooker seems to be displaying what we might term 'a stream of consciousness'.
14. Genesis 21.9–10; Hebrews 11.24–25.
15. Jude 18.
16. Romans 10.2–4; Acts 17.22.
17. Titus 3.11.
18. Hooker is most probably referring here to exiled Roman Catholics.
19. Colossians 1.21–23.
20. Hooker constructs this beautiful prayer from a variety of sources in the Bible, including Colossians 3; Romans 6.11; Ephesians 2.2, 4–5; 2 Timothy 3.2–4; Psalms 131.2; 1 Kings 3; 2 Chronicles 3; John 6.33; Revelation 15.2–3.
21. Here is our only firm clue to the dating of the sermons in Jude. The event Hooker refers to as having occurred 24 years earlier is probably the accession of Elizabeth I to the throne in 1558. That fixes this sermon at 1582 or 1583. See Laetitia Yeandle's analysis in the *Folger Edition*, V, 1–2.
22. Matthew 16.18 and John 21.20–23. Hooker is stretching a point here. Christ seems quite definitive about founding His Church on *petrus*, the rock, whereas Scripture specifically denies that He meant that His disciple would never die.
23. Hooker is referring here to Mary Queen of Scots as the Pope's idea of a 'virtuous' ruler and Elizabeth I as the Pope's idea of a 'strumpet'.
24. Richard Bristow was a sixteenth-century Roman Catholic Divine whose writings were circulated illegally in England.

— 3 —
Building Up the Faith[1]

✷

In this sermon Hooker extols God's unfailing love for His children. Faith is all that is required to receive God's unending mercy. We build up and retain this faith primarily through Christ's Church. For Hooker, the Papacy was a major threat to the true Church and therefore to faith itself.

> ***But you, my friends, should remember the predictions made by the apostles of our Lord Jesus Christ. This was the warning they gave you: 'In the final age there will be men [mockers] who pour scorn on religion, and follow their own godless lusts. These men draw a line between spiritual and unspiritual persons, although they are themselves wholly unspiritual. But you, my friends, must [fortify] edify yourselves in your most sacred faith. Continue to pray in the power of the Holy Spirit. Keep yourselves in the love of God, and look forward to the day when our Lord Jesus Christ in his mercy will give eternal life.*** Jude 17–21 (NEB)

— *God Loves His Own* —

Having spoken elsewhere on Jude's words about mockers who will come in the later days and backsliders who fell from the faith, I am now, with the help of God and His Good Spirit, going to lay before you the meaning of these words of exhortation.

In the first place, anyone who has eyes to see only need open them to perceive how the Lord cares for His children, how desirous He is to see them profit and grow up to the stature of Christ, how loath to have them misled in any way, either by examples of wicked people or worldly enticements, provocations of the flesh, or any other efforts to deceive them and estrange their hearts from God.

God never reaches the point in His relationship with us where He cares not whether we sink or swim. No! He has written our names in the palm of His hand. In the ring on His finger our names are engraved in sentences not only of mercy but also of judgement. Whenever God denounces the wicked, He makes some proviso for His children, as if they were privileged persons. 'Touch not my anointed servants, do my Prophets no harm. Do no damage to sea or land or trees until we have set the seal of our God upon the foreheads of His servants.'[2] Whenever He speaks of godless men He joins words of comfort to those of admonition or exhortation whereby we are moved to rest and settle our hearts in Him.

In the third chapter of the second letter of Timothy, the Apostle says that evil men and deceivers shall wax worse and worse, deceiving and being deceived. But we should continue in the ways we have learned. In chapter six of Timothy's first letter, we read that 'there are some men who, in reaching for money, have strayed from the faith and spiked themselves with thorny griefs. But you, man of God, must shun all this and pursue justice, piety, fidelity, love, patience, and meekness.'[3]

In St Paul's second letter to the Thessalonians, we read that God sends strong delusions to those who have not accepted, in love, the truth that can save them in order that they will believe lies. But, says Paul, 'we ought always to thank God for you brothers and sisters who are loved by the Lord because God has chosen you for salvation, through sanctification of the spirit and faith in the truth.'[4]

In today's Epistle from St Jude, we read that there shall come mockers in the final days, walking after their own ungodly lusts. Being beloved of God, however, we are to 'fortify and edify ourselves in our most sacred faith'.

All of these sweet exhortations which God put everywhere in the mouths of the Prophets and Apostles of Jesus Christ are evident tokens that God does not sit in heaven, careless and unmindful of our condition. Can a mother forget her child? Surely a mother will hardly forget her child.[5] Even if a mother is unnatural and forgets the fruit of her womb, still God's judgements show plainly that He cannot forget those whose hearts He framed and fashioned anew in simplicity and truth to serve and love Him.

When the wickedness of man was so great and the earth so filled with cruelty that it could no longer endure God's righteousness, God could not restrain His wrathful words from bursting forth like wine from a bottle that has no opening: 'My spirit can struggle and strive no longer; an end of all flesh shall come before me.'[6] Even then God chose Noah, who had found grace in God's eyes. He said to Noah, 'I will establish my covenant with you. You shall go into the ark, with your sons and your wife and your sons' wives.'

Do we not see, in the 19th chapter of Genesis, what arrangement God made for Lot and his family lest the fiery destruction of the wicked should overtake him? Overnight, the angels made inquiry as to what sons, daughters and sons-in-law, what wealth and substance Lot had. God seemed to stand in a kind of fear, lest something or other of Lot's would be left behind. His will was that nothing that Lot had, not a hoof of any beast, not a thread of any garment, should be singed with that great fire.

Despite all this, Lot lingered, until at length angels had to take him and his wife by their arms and carry them outside the city.[7]

Was ever any father so careful to save his child from the flame? One would think that being told to escape the city for his life and not to look back or tarry on the plain, but to hasten to the mountains and save himself, Lot would do so gladly. Yet, behold, he is so far from having a cheerful and willing heart to do whatever God commanded him to do for his own good, that he argues with God as though God was mistaken in sending him to the hills where he fears he might die rather than saving him within a nearby city. God is willing to yield to this condition, saying that He 'will spare this city but can do nothing' till Lot comes out of it.

God can do nothing? Yes, but not because of any weakness in Him (for who is comparable to the Lord in power?) but because of the greatness of His mercy which would not allow Him to lift up

His arm against that city within which His righteous servant had a fancy to remain. O the depth of the riches of the mercy and love of God! God is afraid to offend us who are not afraid to displease Him!

God can do nothing until He has saved us who find in our hearts anything other than the impulse to serve Him. Yet it will not content Him to exempt us from the pit that is dug for the wicked or to comfort us when mention is made of the fate of the reprobates and the godless or to save us as the apples of his eye when fire comes down from heaven to consume the inhabitants of the earth – unless every Prophet, every Apostle and every servant He sends forth in His name comes before Him laden with this and similar exhortations: 'O beloved, build up yourselves in your most holy faith; give yourselves over to prayer; keep yourselves in the love of God; look for the mercy of our Lord Jesus Christ unto eternal life.'[8]

'Edify yourselves.' This phrase is borrowed from the builder's trade but must be understood spiritually, in a metaphorical sense. We see such figures of speech throughout Scripture. In the sixth chapter of John's Gospel we are told that in the desert our fathers' mouths watered for bodily food but God gave them manna as 'bread from heaven'. Our Saviour, turning their appetite in a new direction, told them, 'I am the bread of life, he that comes to me shall not hunger and [. . .] thirst.' In the sixth chapter of Matthew, Christ tells us to 'lay up treasures for ourselves in heaven'. Paul, in First Timothy chapter 2, refers to the vanity of certain women, saying that they should 'clothe themselves with shamefulness and modesty' and 'put on the apparel of good works'. [. . .] These are the ornaments, the bracelets and jewels which enflame the love of Christ and set His heart on fire for His spouse [the Church].[9]

— *We are God's Holy Temple* —

Perhaps Jude is exhorting us not to build our houses but to build up ourselves because he foresees, by the spirit of the Almighty that was in him, that there would be people in the last days as there were in the first, who will encourage and stir up each other to make brick, and fire it, and build houses as huge as cities and towers as high as heaven in order to get a name for themselves. They would evict the poor and the fatherless and the widow and build places of rest for dogs and swine in their rooms and make stables of places where God's people had worshipped the Lord. Surely this is the vanity of all vanities, one that is a widespread sickness of this age.

What it all will mean I do not know, except that God has set His people to work to provide fuel against that day when the Lord Jesus Christ shall show Himself from heaven with His mighty angels – in flaming fire. As Solomon says, 'what good comes to the owners of these earthly things beyond the beholding of them with their eyes?' 'Martha, Martha, you busy yourself about many things. One thing [only] is necessary.'[10]

You are too busy, my brothers, with timber and brick. You who choose to build yourselves up choose the better course. You are the temples of the living God who said, 'I will dwell in them and will walk in them, and they shall be my people, and I will be their God.'[11]

Which of you will gladly remain or abide in a misshapen or broken-down house? Shall we then allow sin and vanity to drop into our eyes and ears and every corner of our bodies and souls, knowing that we are the temples of the Holy Ghost? Which of you receives a guest whom he honours or loves and does not clean his chamber before the guest comes? Shall we allow the chamber of our hearts and consciences to be full of vomit, full of filth, full of garbage, knowing that Christ has said, 'I and my Father will come and dwell with you'? Is it proper for your oxen to lie in parlours and yourselves to lodge in animal cribs? Is it seemly 'for you to dwell in your fine houses, and the house of the Almighty lie in waste – a house you yourselves are?'[12]

Do our eyes not behold how God every day overtakes the wicked in their journeys and how suddenly they pop down into the pit of hell; how God's judgements for their crimes come so swiftly upon them that they have not the leisure to cry out: 'Alas!' How their lives are cut off in a moment like a thread; how they pass like a shadow; how they open their mouths to speak and God takes them right in the middle of a vain or idle word? Dare we lay down, take our rest, and eat our meals, securely and carelessly in the midst of such great and extensive ruin?

— *Holy Communion* —

Blessed and praised for ever be God's name, who, knowing of what senseless and heavy metal we are made, has instituted in His Church a spiritual supper, a Holy Communion, to be celebrated often so that we might by that celebration have the frequent occasion to examine these buildings of ours and see in what condition they stand. Since God does not dwell in temples that are unclean, we receive this holy supper as a seal, a promise that we are His house, His sanctuary; that His Christ is as truly united to me as I to Him – as my arm is united to my shoulder; that He dwells in me as truly as the elements of bread and wine abide within me; that by receiving these awful mysteries, I profess my faith.

If this profession is honest, then we receive divine comfort, but if we act hypocritically, then woe unto us.

Therefore, before we put forth our hands to take this blessed Sacrament, we are charged to examine and test our hearts to see whether God is truly in us or not. If by faith and unfeigned love, we are found to be temples of the Holy Ghost, then we should judge whether we have tended to the upkeep of our building so that the Spirit dwelling within us has in no way been vexed, molested, or grieved. If the Holy Spirit has been abused – and, no doubt, even in the best and most nearly perfect among us this sometimes happens because of our lack of faith, failure to show charity, lack of zeal, and wrong-doing in our lives – oh, then, fly to God with honest repentance, fall down before Him, beg Him for whatever is necessary to repair your decay before you fall into that desolation of which the Prophet spoke when he said, 'Your breach is great like the sea; who can heal you?'

When we receive the Sacrament of the Supper of the Lord in this spiritual way, is not all other wine like the water of Marah compared to this blessed cup? Is not manna like gall and our holy bread like manna? Is there not a taste of Christ Jesus in the heart of him who eats this Supper? Does not he who drinks behold plainly in this cup that his soul is bathed in the blood of the Lamb?

Oh, beloved in our Lord and Saviour Jesus Christ, if you would taste how sweet the Lord is, if you would receive the King of Glory, then first build up yourselves.

Young men, I say this to you, for you are His house. By faith, you are conquerors of Satan and can overcome evil. *Fathers*, I am speaking to you also. You are His house because you have known Him. *Sweet babies*, I speak even to you, for you also are His house because your sins are forgiven for His sake. *Mothers, wives, and sisters*, I withhold nothing from you, for you also are the Lord's building, and, as St Peter says, you are 'heirs of the grace of life' as surely as we men.[13] Although you are not permitted to speak out in public church assemblies, yet you must be inquisitive about this building of God's, especially at home with your husbands and friends. Be not as Delilah was with Samson, but as Sarah was with Abraham. You are the daughters of Sarah so long as you do good works and build up yourselves in the faith.

Having spoken thus far about the exhortation whereby we are called upon to edify and to build ourselves, it now remains to consider the thing prescribed, namely, what is it that is to be built?

— *Building Up Our Faith* —

That which is prescribed, that which we are to build, is our faith. That is the foundation of the building. We might say that it is the first link in a chain of many links. If you pull the first, you draw the rest along. Or we might imagine a ladder with many rungs. If you take away the lowest, all hope of ascending to the highest is removed. Similarly, because all the teachings and promises in God's law and Christ's Gospel hang upon the command: believe! and because the last of God's graces flows from the first, namely, that He glorifies none that He has not justified nor justifies any but those He has called to a true and lively faith in Christ Jesus, St Jude, in exhorting us to 'build yourselves', expressly names only one thing wherein we may be edified, namely, faith. Faith is the ground and the glory of all that is worthy in this building.

The Apostle Paul says in Ephesians:

> Thus you are no longer aliens in a foreign land, but fellow-citizens with God's people, members of God's household. You are built upon the foundation laid by the apostles and prophets, and Christ Jesus himself is the foundation-stone. In him the whole building is bonded together and grows into a holy temple in the Lord. In him you too are being built with all the rest into a spiritual dwelling for God. [14]

The strength of every building that is of God rests not in anyone's arms or legs but only on our faith, even as the valour of Samson lay only in his hair. This is the reason why we are so earnestly called upon to edify ourselves in faith. It is not as if this bare action of our minds, whereby we believe in the Gospel of Christ, is able in itself to make us invincible like the stone which abides in a building for ever and will not collapse. No! It is not the worthiness of our believing but the virtue of Him in whom we believe by which we stand as solidly as a house built upon a rock.

We learn from the Apostle, in the tenth chapter of the first letter to the Corinthians, not only that, being supported by faith in Christ, we receive all our strength and fitness from Him, but also, that this strength and fitness is no cause for us to be high-minded or to fail to work out our salvation with a reverent, trembling, and holy fear. If you boast of your faith, remember that Christ chose His Apostles. They did not choose Him. Every heart must think and every tongue must speak, 'Not unto us, O Lord, not unto us, nor to anything which is in us, but unto Your Name only belongs all the praise for the treasures and riches of every temple which is of God.' This should exclude all boasting and vaunting of our faith.

But the fact that God chose us should not make us careless about the continuing need to build up, to edify, ourselves in faith. True, it is the Lord who delivers our souls, but only when we put our trust in His mercy. It is God who gives us eternal life, but only if we believe in His Son.

If you desire to know more about how necessary for us it is to edify and build up ourselves in faith, mark the words of the blessed Apostle: 'Without faith it is impossible to please God.'[15] If I offer to God all the sheep and oxen that there are in the world, all the temples built from the day of Adam until this hour, if I break my very heart with calling upon God, and wear out my tongue with preaching, if I sacrifice my body and my soul to Him and have not faith, it all comes to nothing. Without faith it is impossible to please God. Our Lord and Saviour, being asked in the sixth chapter of John's Gospel how we can do the will of God, answered, 'This is the work that God requires: believe in the one whom he has sent.'[16]

What proof do we need to look for that no work of ours, no building up of ourselves can in any way be profitable to us unless we build up our faith? Look at Israel, once the chosen and special people of God, to whom were given the covenants of mercy, the Law of Moses, the services of God, the promises of Jesus. They were not only the offspring of Abraham, father of the faithful, but Christ Himself was their offspring. Blessed be God for evermore. [...]

— *Tearing Down the Faith: The Bishop of Rome* —

A strange and strong delusion it is with which that man of sin, the Pope, has bewitched the world. A powerful spirit of error it is which has brought men to such a senseless and unreasonable persuasion that men clothed with mortality and sin, as we are, can do God such service as shall make a full and perfect satisfaction before the seat of God, and more satisfaction even than is necessary for themselves. Also, it is a delusion that anyone, by the hand of a bishop of Rome, a Pope, for such and such a price may buy the surplus of others' merits, purchase the fruits of others' labours, and build up his soul by another's faith. Is not this man [the Pope] drowned in the gall of bitterness? Is his heart right in the sight of God? Can he have any fellowship with Peter and with the successors of Peter when he has such evil ideas about building up the precious Temple of the Holy Ghost? Let his money perish with him and he with it because he judges that the gift of God may be sold for money.[17]

Beloved in the Lord, do not deceive yourselves or allow yourselves to be deceived. You can no more receive comfort for your souls by another's faith than warmth for your bodies from another's clothes, or sustenance by the bread that another eats. As Tertullian said, 'The just shall live by his own faith. Let a saint, yes even a martyr, be content to cleanse himself of his own sins.'[18] Did ever anyone, except the Son of God, by his death deliver another from death? (Christ indeed was able to provide safe conduct for a thief from the Cross to Paradise. For this purpose He came, that, being Himself pure from sin, He might take on the sins of others.) You who suppose that you can do what Christ did and justify another person by your righteousness, lay down your life for your brother. Die for me! But if, like me, you are a sinner, how can the oil of your lamp be sufficient both for you and me?

Let this be noted, therefore, as the first principle of how you are to edify ourselves: you can only be edified by your own most holy faith.

As St Jude said, our faith is something very holy because by it we are justified. Being justified, all our iniquities are covered over. God sees us in the righteousness that is imputed by our faith, not in the sins that we have committed. It is true that we are full of sin, both original and actual. If we deny this we are double sinners, for we are both sinners and liars. To deny sin is plainly and clearly to prove it, because if we say we have no sin, we lie and by lying, prove that we have sinned.

God's gift of righteousness covers the sins of every soul who is a believer. God, by pardoning our sin, has taken it away so that now, although our transgressions are multiplied beyond the hairs on our head, yet, being justified, we are as free and clear as if there were not one spot of stain or any uncleanness in us.

Sin being removed, we are made into the righteous of God in Christ. David, speaking about this righteousness, said, 'Blessed is the man whose iniquities are forgiven.'[19] No one is blessed except through God's righteousness. Everyone whose sin is taken away is blessed. Therefore, everyone whose sin is covered over becomes the righteousness of God in Christ. This righteousness allows us to appear holy and pure and blameless in the presence of God.

This, then, is the sum of what I am saying: faith justifies; justification washes away sin; once sin is removed, we are clothed by God with righteousness; righteousness makes us holy. To make a wicked and sinful man holy through his faith is more than to create a world out of nothing.

Oh, that our hearts were stretched out like tents and that the eyes of our understanding were as bright as the sun so that we might thoroughly know the riches of the glorious inheritance of Saints and what the exceeding greatness of God's power towards us is – we whom He accepts as pure and holy because of our belief in Him.

Oh, that the Lord would give this doctrine entry to the stony and brazen heart of the Jew, who seeks righteousness, but not of faith. Hence, the Jews stumble at belief in Christ, and so are bruised, split to pieces like a ship that has run herself upon the rocks. Oh, that God would cast down the eyes of the proud and humble the souls of the high-minded so that they might, at length, abhor the garments of their own flesh, which cannot hide their nakedness, and put on the faith of Christ Jesus. [. . .] Oh, that God would open the Ark of His mercy wherein His doctrine lies and set it wide open before the eyes of poor afflicted consciences which fly up and down upon the water of their afflictions and can see nothing but the gulf and deluge of their sins and no place therein to rest their feet.

The God of pity and compassion give you all strength and courage every day and every hour and every moment to build and edify yourselves in this most pure and holy faith.

— *The Church* —

Before I lay this matter of faith to rest and turn to the second branch of my discourse, which is prayer,[20] I must add something about how we should apply our faith to others and to ourselves.

For your better understanding of Jude's exhortation to 'edify yourselves', you should note that every church and congregation consists of a multitude of believers, just as every house is built of many stones. The nature of the mystical body of the Church is such that it allows no distinction among its invisible members, whether it be Paul or Apollos, prince, or prophet, one that is taught or one who teaches. All are equally Christ's and Christ is equally theirs. But in the external administration of the Church, since God is not the author of confusion, but of peace, it is necessary that within each congregation there be a distinction, not of inner worth, but of outward status.

The Church, therefore, in terms of its ecclesiastical administration, consists of two sorts of people: those who are ministered to and those to whom the work of ministry is committed – the pastors whom the Holy Ghost has made overseers of the flock. If the guide of the congregation, whatever may be his title or certification, is diligent in his vocation, feeding the flock that depends on him, caring for it, not because he must but willingly, not for filthy money but out of a keen mind, not as though he were a tyrant but as an example to the flock, guiding them wisely; and, if the people, for their part, yield themselves to the pattern of truth shown to them, not like a rough stone or flint refusing to be smoothed or squared for the building; and, if the government carefully and diligently surveys the whole order of the Church, providing by statute and bodily punishment, if necessary, that all things are done under a fair rule of law (even as Moses provided that all things be done according to the pattern he had seen on the mountain), then, of such a congregation, everyone will say: 'Behold a people that are wise, a people that walk in the statutes and ordinances of their God, a people full of knowledge and understanding, a people that have the skill to build up themselves [in the faith].'[21]

We see now how fruitless this exhortation has been for those who bend all their labour to build and manage the papacy, without any care for building up themselves in faith. When God's people inquired of the Roman priests, 'What shall we do to have eternal life? How shall we build and edify ourselves?' they were laden down with doctrines that are the precepts of men, not God. They were told to tire themselves with bodily exercises, ordered to do things that God never required of them, and never told what God did require of them. Their eyes were fed with pictures and their ears filled with melodies but their souls withered, starved, and pined away. They cry for bread, and behold, stones are offered them. They ask for fish, and, behold, they have scorpions in their hands. You see, O Lord, that these papist priests build themselves – but not in faith. They feed their children, but not with holy food. Their shameful rulers say, 'Bring,' and not 'Build.'

God is righteous and is aware of their stinking drunkenness, their abominations, their madness. The wind has bound them up in her wings and they shall be ashamed of their actions.

If there is any feeling of Christ, any drop of heavenly dew, any spark of God's spirit within you, stir it up. Be careful to build up and edify yourselves first, then the flock. I say first yourselves because he who would set the hearts of others on fire with the love of Christ must first himself burn with love.

It is our own lack of faith, my brothers and sisters, which makes us inadequate in building up others in the faith. Why is this? It is because our own desires are misplaced. We are like those women who have a longing to eat coal and lime and filth. We are well fed, some of us with honour, some with ease, some with wealth. By comparison, the Gospel can seem loathsome and unpleasant to our taste. How, then, can we feed others that holy food which we do not fancy ourselves? If faith waxes cold and slender in the heart of the Prophet, it will soon perish from the ears of the people. [. . .]

I ask you who are a part of the residue of God's elect and chosen people: who is there among you that has taken a survey of the house of God, as it was in the day of Jesus' blessed Apostles, and seen this holy temple, the Church, in her first glory? How do you see her today? Is it not by comparison, almost nothing? When you look upon those who have undertaken the charge of your souls and realize how far they have strayed from the standard set for them, how few there are who tread the steps of their ancient predecessors, you are filled with indignation and easily drawn to the complaints which point to the difference (which we bewail) between present and former times. We are easily persuaded that those who lived and enjoyed those days that are now gone were happy compared to us who have succeeded them. Were not their bishops irreprovable, wise, righteous, holy, temperate, well thought of, even by those outside the Church? Were not their pastors, guides and teachers able and willing to teach wholesome doctrine and to try to correct whatever threatened the truth? Were their priests made from the refuse of the people? Were men like the children of Nineveh, who were unable to discern between the right hand and the left, put in charge of congregations? Did teachers abandon the flocks over which the Holy Ghost had made them overseers? Did their prophets take over holy places like spoils, without a reverent calling? Were their leaders so unkindly disposed toward them that they could find it in their hearts to sell them like sheep or oxen, not caring how they treated them?

Beloved, do not deceive yourselves. As St Gregory says, if the faults of your pastors and guides offend you, it is your own fault that they are so faulty. Whenever you have an evil governor, accuse yourself, not him. His being this way is what you deserve. The only way to repair the ruins, breaches, and offensive decay in others is to begin the reformation of yourselves. [22]

That we may all sincerely, seriously, and speedily do so, may God the Father grant, for His Son our Saviour Jesus' sake, unto whom, with the Holy Ghost, three persons, one eternal everlasting God, be honour and glory and praise for ever. Amen.

Notes

1. This sermon is traditionally named 'The Second Sermon on Jude'.
2. Psalms 105.15; Revelation 7.3.
3. 1 Timothy 6.10–11.

4. 2 Thessalonians 2.11–13.
5. Is Hooker referring to his own mother here? He may have known her only briefly when he was a small boy and nurtured a fear that she had never really known him. See Philip B. Secor, *Richard Hooker Prophet of Anglicanism* (Burns & Oates, Tunbridge Wells, 1999), 6–10.
6. Job 32.19–20; Genesis 6.3, 13; 6.8, 18.
7. Genesis 19.12, 15.
8. Jude 21–22.
9. John 6.31, 34, 35; Matthew 6.20; 1 Timothy 2.9–10; Ephesians 6.14; Ezekiel 16.11.
10. Ecclesiastes 5.10; Luke 10.41–42.
11. 2 Corinthians 6.16.
12. John 14.23; Haggai 1.4.
13. 1 John 2.12–13; 1 Peter 3.7.
14. Ephesians 2.19–22 (NEB).
15. Hebrews 11.16.
16. John 6.28–29 (NEB).
17. Acts 8.20–23.
18. Tertullian, *De Pudicitia*, 22.4, *Opera Omnia*, 1584, p. 1214; *On Modesty*, *The Ante-Nicene Fathers*, 4.100, cited in W. Speed Hill, gen. ed., *The Folger Library Edition of the Works of Richard Hooker* Vols I–V (The Belknap Press of Harvard University, Cambridge, MA and London, 1977–1990), V, 697.
19. Psalms 32.1.
20. Hooker may be referring to his sermon on Matthew 7.7, reproduced in this volume as 'The Pathway to God'.
21. Deuteronomy 4.6–8.
22. Gregory I, *Expositio*, chapter 25, *Opera Omnia*, 1551, f.148r.

— 4 —
Grace and Righteousness[1]

This is the most theological of Hooker's sermons and tractates. It deals with the manner of achieving God's grace in the form of righteousness. The great issue of the Reformation – are we justified by faith or works? – is the central question under discussion. Hooker's distinction between justification and sanctification as a way of unravelling the faith–works controversy has remained an important ingredient in Anglican theology ever since.

The tractates were delivered as sermons at the Temple Church in late 1585 or early 1586, as part of Hooker's great 'Temple Debate' with his cousin, the arch-Calvinist Walter Travers. Recently appointed by the Queen as Master of the Temple, each Sunday morning Hooker would deliver his sermon. Each Sunday afternoon, Travers, who was Reader at the Temple and aspired to Hooker's post, would give a sermon in which he attempted to refute Hooker's ideas. These debates were of importance because the Temple Church, located in the Inns of Court, just off Fleet Street, was one of the most influential pulpits in England, serving most of the lawyers and judges and many of the political leaders and merchants residing in London. (Only St Paul's was more important.) In the next century, the historian Thomas Fuller was to say of this exchange: 'The Pulpit rang pure Canterbury in the morning and pure Geneva in the afternoon.'

The most controversial of Hooker's themes in these sermons were those which, in various ways, seemed to express approval for the Roman Catholic Church and its members, especially his claim that Roman Catholics who had lived before the Reformation might be saved because they had not sinned intentionally, and therefore a merciful God might forgive them their errors. Even the Pope might find mercy from God. Such ideas, so harmless to our ears, were dangerous in the mouth of a prominent church figure like Hooker during these years of threat to the Queen and the nation from Catholics within and outside the realm. These were years that saw the execution of

Mary Stuart, Queen of Scots, within two years of the delivery of these sermons, for her part in Catholic conspiracies against Elizabeth, and near hysteria throughout the country over the impending invasion, in the name of the Pope and the Catholic religion, from Spain.

Hooker takes as his text, Habakkuk. He seems to have preferred drawing on this Old Testament Prophet for the same reason that he liked using St Jude from the New Testament. Both writers dealt with a problem that deeply troubled Hooker: how to respond to serious threats to the faith, order, and peace of the Church that came from many of those charged with leading the Church – in Hooker's case, advanced Calvinist ministers and theologians like Walter Travers, Thomas Cartwright, John Field and others, who, in the name of reformation, were, in Hooker's opinion, spreading misleading, if not false, doctrine.

These sermons precipitated Travers' efforts to use his considerable influence with the Queen's chief minister, the Lord Treasurer, William Burleigh, to have Hooker removed from the Temple and himself installed as Master there. Although that attempt failed – Travers was the one removed – Hooker's reputation as a rising figure in the church hierarchy may have been damaged by the public exchange with Travers, simply because the Queen greatly disliked controversialists in her Church and Hooker had been unable to keep the peace at the Temple Church.

The wicked outwit the righteous, and so justice comes out perverted. Habakkuk 1.4 (NEB)

For a clearer understanding of the Prophet's meaning here, we should first consider the question of who these wicked people are who are encompassing the righteous, next, who these righteous people are, and finally, what is meant by perverse judgements.

Touching upon the first question, there are two kinds of wicked men of whom the blessed Apostle speaks when he writes to the Corinthians, 'What business of mine is it to judge outsiders? God is their judge. You are judges within the fellowship. Root out the evil-doer from your community.'[2] Thus there are wicked people within the Church whom the Church may judge, and wicked people outside the Church whom God alone judges.

When particular persons within the Church are apparently wicked and cannot otherwise be reformed, the Apostle's rule is that we separate them from ourselves. If, however, whole assemblies are wicked, we are to separate ourselves from them. Light cannot co-exist with darkness. The wicked whom Habakkuk referred to were the Babylonians who were people outside the Church. We have often heard in what negative ways he urged God to judge them.

— *Righteousness* —

Concerning the righteous, there neither is nor ever was any purely natural person who was absolutely righteous, devoid of all unrighteousness, of all sin. We dare not exempt from this truth even the Blessed Virgin herself. Even she, the Mother of the Redeemer, is not, apart from Christ's redemption of her, released from the bond of that ancient sin. If Christ paid a ransom for all, even for her, it follows that all without exception are captives to sin and that no one is righteous in himself.

We are, however, absolutely righteous in Christ. (Unless the world can produce a Christian, it cannot show us a perfectly righteous person.) In Christ we have wisdom, justice, sanctification and redemption: wisdom because He revealed His Father's will to us; justice because He offered Himself as a sacrifice for our sins; sanctification, because He has given us His Spirit; redemption, because He has appointed a day to deliver His children out of the bondage of corruption into a glorious liberty.

How Christ is made our wisdom and our redemption, I may discuss on some other occasion, but how He is made our righteousness I will explain now.

In the world to come there is a glorifying righteousness for mankind. In this world there is a justifying and sanctifying righteousness. The righteousness that will clothe us in the world to come is both perfect and inherent in us. The righteousness in this world whereby we are justified is perfect but not inherent, and the righteousness whereby we are sanctified is inherent but not perfect.

With this distinction in mind we have a path for understanding the great controversial issue between us and the Church of Rome concerning the matter of righteousness and how that justifies us. In the first place, the Church of Rome imagines that the mother of our Lord and Saviour Jesus Christ was, for His sake and by special protection, free from all sin. Concerning all the rest, they teach as we do that everyone has sinned. This includes infants who have never actually offended anyone but are nevertheless defiled in their very natures, devoid of justice and separated from God.

Rome teaches, as we do, that God alone justifies our souls, without any other cause for this justification but God's will. Nothing in us causes God to do this. The papists also teach, with us, that only through Christ's merits is anyone justified. They teach, as we do, that although Christ, as God, is the cause of our justification, yet there is something required of us. God is the cause of our natural life. He also gives life to the soul within our body and His merit makes this life just. But just as medicine made for health does not heal simply by being made, so, by Christ's merits, justification does not come about until it is actually applied to us. To this extent, we join hands with this Church of Rome.

— *Justification* —

Where, then, do we disagree with Rome? We differ about the nature of the very essence of the medicine whereby Christ cures our disease, about the manner in which He applies that medicine, and about the number and power of the actions God requires of us for the effective application of the righteousness that will comfort our souls. When the Romans are required to show just what that righteousness is that justifies a Christian, they answer that it is a divine, spiritual quality – a quality which once received into the soul, first converts a person to be God's own and secondly gives that person the power to bring forth such works as are performed by those who are born of Him. This operates, they say, in the same manner as when the soul, being joined to the body, makes one a reasonable creature, capable of performing the natural function proper to his kind. Thus does the soul become gracious and amiable in the sight of God.

They wrongly call this *grace* in that by its power they believe that we are purged, purified, washed clean of all the stains and pollutions of sin, and enabled, through the merit of Christ, to be delivered from sin and eternal death and condemnation which is the reward of sin. They see this grace applied by a kind of infusion that empowers the soul, so that, even as the body is warmed by heat within itself, the soul is righteous by a kind of inherent grace to become more and more justified by doing good works. As the body may become warmer by more heat so the soul may become more and more justified by doing good works. Thereby, the Church of Rome says that the first receipt of grace brings the first divine justification, but thereafter, a second kind of justification comes through an earned increase of God's grace – earned by the merit of good works.

In like manner the papists believe that grace and hence justification can be decreased by the demerits of venal sins and lost altogether by commission of mortal sins. Since it is necessary in the first case to repair and in the second to restore the loss of righteousness, the initial infusion of grace has within it various means of applying new infusions. Hence they apply grace to infants through Baptism, without either faith or works. (In infants this truly does take away original sin and any requisite punishment.) They also apply grace to infidels and wicked persons, first by justification in Baptism without works but not without faith. In this case both original and actually committed sins, as well as eternal and temporal punishments, are taken away. To those who attain the first justification, i.e., the first receipt of grace, grace may be increased by good works. These good works yield a second justification. If the sinners do yet more good works, then more grace is received and thus they are more and more justified.

If there has been a diminution of grace through commission of venal sins, the Romans simply apply holy water and require Ave Marias, crossings, papal salutations, and such like, as reparations for grace decayed. If grace has been lost altogether through a mortal sin, then the Church of Rome applies the sacrament, as they call it, of penance, which they claim has the power to confer grace anew. This new grace is not as strong as the original grace because it only cleanses the stain or guilt of the sin committed and changes the punishment from an eternal to a satisfactory temporal punishment. If there is not enough time in one's life to receive all of the temporal punishments, then one must endure them in the afterlife, with the proviso that the punishments may be lightened by attending Masses, performing works of charity, going on holy pilgrimages, or enduring fasts, or that punishments may be shortened or removed altogether by papal pardons.

This is the mystery of this man of sin, the Pope, namely this maze that the Church of Rome causes her followers to thread when they ask the ways of justification. I cannot today rip apart this building and sift it piece by piece. I will only say a few words by way of fashioning from the teaching of the Apostles a different kind of structure.

The Apostle Paul said, 'Undoubtedly, I count all things loss and judge them to be dung that I may win Christ and be found in Him, not having my own righteousness, but that which is, through the faith of Christ, the righteousness which is of God, through faith.'[3]

Whether the papists speak of their first or second justification, they make the essence of it a divine and inherent quality – a righteousness – which is within us. If it is in us, then it is ours, even as our souls are ours and even though we have them from God and for only so long as it pleases Him. If He withdraws the breath of life from our nostrils, we fall to dust. The righteousness wherein we must be found if we are to be justified is not our own. Therefore, we cannot be justified by any inherent quality. Christ alone merited righteousness and He for as many others as are 'found to be in Him'. In Christ, God finds us if we are faithful for by faith alone we are incorporated into Him. Then, although in ourselves we are altogether sinful and unrighteous, being found in Christ, no matter how impious and full of iniquity and sin we are, through faith and repentance we are seen by God with a gracious eye and accepted, pardoned, and made righteous in Christ as though we had never sinned at all. In the sight of God we are perfectly righteous in Christ as though we had fulfilled all of His commandments. As the Apostle says, 'God made Him who knew no sin to become sin itself for our sake so that we might become the righteousness of God in Him.' And such we are in the sight of God, just as is His very own Son. Let others count all this as our folly, frenzy or fury, or whatever. It is our wisdom and our comfort. We care for no knowledge in the world but this: that man sinned and God suffered, that God made Himself the sin of man, and that men are made the righteousness of God.[4]

You see, therefore, that the Church of Rome, in teaching justification by inherent grace, perverts the truth of Christ. From the Apostles we have received a very different teaching.

— *Sanctification* —

The righteousness of sanctification is different from the righteousness of justification. We do not deny that the righteousness of sanctification is inherent and that we must work to achieve it. We are righteous in one way by the faith of Abraham and in the other by the works of Abraham. Of the one way St Paul says, 'To him who does no works but believes, faith yields righteousness.' On the other hand, St John says, 'He is righteous who does the works of righteousness.' St Paul shows that by Abraham's example we have righteousness by faith without works. But St James says that by Abraham's example one is justified by works along with faith. We see that St Paul clearly severs these two aspects of Christian righteousness from one another in the second chapter of Romans where he writes, 'Being freed from sin and made servants of God you have your fruits in holiness and, at the end, everlasting life.'[5]

The Prophet Habakkuk, in our text, calls the Jews righteous not only because they were justified by faith, and so free from sin, but also because they had their measure of the *fruit of holiness*. (We must be charitable to the Jews at this point and leave it to God to judge what His people are really like. We must speak of all others in the terms they use to describe themselves. Every Christian person knows that with Christian charity one should think and speak of his brothers and sisters as people who have in full measure the *fruit of holiness* and a right to whatever titles God may have bestowed as special favours and mercies to his chosen servants – in this case, the Jews.) In this sense we note that the Apostles everywhere use the word 'saints' and 'the righteous.' So let us all endeavour to be such as we wish to be called.

Even if we have the 'fruits of holiness,' we must remember that the more we seem to abound therein, the more need we have to be strengthened and supported. Our very virtues may be snares to entrap us. The enemy that waits for any occasion to work our ruin has always found it harder to overthrow a humble sinner than a proud saint. There is no one's position so dangerous as his whom Satan has persuaded that his own righteousness shall present him pure and blameless in the sight of God.

If we could say that we are not guilty of anything at all in our consciences, should we not still plead guilty before the presence of God, who sees further into our hearts than we ourselves are able to see? If our hands never offered violence to our brothers and sisters, a bloody thought proves us murderers nonetheless. If we never opened our mouths to utter a scandalous, offensive, or hurtful word, the cry of our secret thoughts is heard in the ears of God. And if we do not actually commit the evil deeds we do every day in our thoughts and words, even in the good things that we do, how many defects are intermingled?

God respects our intentions in whatever we do. But when we discount all those 'good deeds' where we have sought our own glory, all those things we do to please other people, or to satisfy our own desires, and those things we do for any reason which is not sincerely and purely for the love of God, a small score is left as the total of our righteous deeds.

Even when the holiest and best deeds we do are considered, we are never more pleasing to God than when we pray. Yet when we pray, how many times are our thoughts distracted? How little reverence do we show to the grand majesty of that God to whom we speak? How little remorse for our own miserable lives? How little taste do we have for the sweet influence of His tender mercy? Are we not often as unwilling to begin and as glad to make an end to our prayers as if God, in saying, 'Call upon Me,' had set before us a burdensome task?

— *God's Grace* —

What I say here may seem somewhat extreme. Therefore, everyone will have to judge my words as his own heart tells him, and in no other way. But I do have one question. If God should say to us (more generously than He did to Abraham when He promised that He would not destroy a city if fifty, forty, thirty, yes, even ten good persons could be found therein), that if He searched all the generations since the fall of Adam and found only one person who had done even one act that marked him pure, without stain or blemish of any kind, that person could serve to ransom all of us and the angels from suffering, do you think that this single human ransom could be found among us mortals?

The best things we do have something in them that requires God's pardon. So how can we do anything truly meritorious and worthy of reward? Indeed, God freely promises a blessed life to all who sincerely keep His Law even if they cannot do so perfectly. So we acknowledge the duty to do our best but renounce any claim that we thereby earn God's grace. God knows that our little *fruit of holiness* is corrupt and unsound. We are to put no confidence in it. We are to challenge nothing in the world because of it. We dare not call God to recognize our works as if we held Him in our debt. Rather, our continual prayer to Him is, and must be, to bear our infirmities and pardon our offences.

But what of the people of whom Habakkuk speaks? Did they all, or at least most of them, try to 'walk uprightly' and did they 'thirst after righteousness'? Did they wish, did they long for the day when 'our ways were made so perfect that we might keep thy statutes'?

No. The words of other Prophets concerning this people show the contrary. How grievously Isaiah mourns over them, 'Ah, sinful nation, people laden with iniquity, wicked seed, corrupt children.'[6]

All of this notwithstanding, the bowels of God's compassion are so wide that He does not turn from us even when we are 'laden with iniquity'. He does not deny us permission to plead with Him that whatever plagues we may deserve we will not be worse off than unbelievers and not hemmed in by pagans and infidels. Jerusalem is a sinful and polluted city, but compared to Babylon it is righteous.

Shall the righteous then be overborne? Shall they be surrounded by the wicked? Habakkuk not only complains that God has treated His people harshly but, in the extremity of the prophet's grief, he strongly infers that God's judgement of His people is perverse.

This inference of Habakkuk contains much that would be important for me to speak about and for you to hear if necessity did not draw me now to another subject. It should not seem burdensome to me or unprofitable to you if I follow the example of Paul and Barnabas and take this opportunity to preach now on a different subject which I have addressed before.

Notes

1. When first published in 1612, this tractate was part of a larger work comprising at least three separate tractates entitled, *A Learned Discourse of Justification, Works, and How the Foundation of Faith is Overthrown*. The other parts deal primarily with the Roman Catholic issue. I have combined those segments in the last sermon in this volume which I have titled 'Faith and Works: Salvation for Roman Catholics'. Not until the nineteenth century were these pieces recognized as Hooker's work. See W. Speed Hill, gen. ed., *The Folger Library Edition of the Works of Richard Hooker* Vols I–V (The Belknap Press of Harvard University, Cambridge, MA and London, 1977–1990), V, 83–104.
2. 1 Corinthians 5.12–13 (NEB).
3. Philippians 3.8–9.
4. 2 Corinthians 11.1, 16–21.
5. Romans 4.5; James 2.21, 24; Romans 6.22; 1 John 3.7.
6. Isaiah 1.4.

— 5 —
Sorrow, Fear and Depression

This sermon is known traditionally as 'A Remedy Against Sorrow and Fear, Delivered in a Funeral Sermon.' Writing three centuries before Sigmund Freud and the birth of modern psychology, Hooker shows remarkable insight into the causes and properties of fear and depression. His word for depression is 'heaviness', but the context in which he uses this word makes it clear that he means a mental state very close to clinical depression. His explanation of the causes and remedies for this debilitating condition may not please all modern clinicians though I suspect many of them will recognize their own theories dressed up (or down) in sixteenth-century religious language. Especially appealing is his prescription of 'patience' as an important (if temporary) remedy for mental and spiritual sickness.

As for fear, Hooker sees this as a healthy, even necessary, human response to danger. In a delightful twist of President Franklin Delano Roosevelt's famous line, 'We have nothing to fear but fear itself,' we hear Hooker say, 'we should fear nothing so much as the extremity of not being afraid.'

We do not know when the sermon was delivered. Because of its pastoral nature, I have placed it during Hooker's tenure at St Mary's, Bishopsbourne, where he served a rural parish and had the opportunity to know his flock intimately enough to preach such a sermon. [1]

The earliest text of the sermon, and the one used here, was printed in 1612 at Oxford on behalf of John Spenser, the President of Corpus Christi College and Hooker's literary executor. It is the second of two sermons on John 14.27 delivered on two different occasions. The first one has not survived. [2]

Let not your heart be troubled, neither let it be afraid.
John 14.27

The holy Apostles, having gathered themselves together by Christ's special instruction and expecting to receive their customary instructions from Him, were told what they had least expected, namely, that the time had come for His departure from this world.

Whereupon they fell into consideration firstly of the many benefits of which his absence would deprive them and secondly of the various evils they would be subjected to once they were deprived of so gracious a master and patron. The one thought overwhelmed their souls with depression, [3] the other with fear.

— *Depression* —

Their Lord and Saviour, whose words had cast down their hearts, presently raised them up again with sentences of sweet encouragement: My dear ones, 'it is for your sakes that I leave the world'. I know the affections of your hearts are tender. But if your love were directed by the wise judgement that should be in you My talk of 'leaving the world and going to My father' would substantially increase 'your joy. Desolate and comfortless I will not leave you.' In spirit, 'I am with you until the world's end.' Whether I am present or absent, nothing shall ever take you out of these hands. My going is in order to take possession not only of what is prepared for Me, but for you also. 'Where I am you shall be.' In the meantime, 'My peace I give you, not as the world gives peace. Let not your heart be troubled neither let it be afraid.' [4]

I have already spoken, in another sermon, about the first part of this sentence from our Lord. Although I wish we were not brought here today on such a sad occasion [a funeral], I will use this opportunity to explore the second part of Christ's statement. In so doing, I trust that what God has ordained [the death of a loved one] may, through his goodness, be turned to your comfort.

By nature, we seek safety from harm. Things that are harmful in the present moment breed depression in us; if anticipated as future events, they cause fear. To abate the one, our Saviour said to His disciples, 'Let not your hearts be troubled.' To moderate the other, He added, 'fear not'.

Grief and depression in the presence of immediate threats cannot help but trouble our minds. It may therefore seem that Christ requires the impossible. Be not troubled? How can we be otherwise? We must note that since it is natural for us to be depressed and fearful in the face of evil, we can be condemned only with reference to the causes of our grief and the extent of it. It is not my purpose to speak at length about all of the ways in which we offend Christ by failing to follow His commandment to fear not and be untroubled, but only to examine the issue as revealed in the lives of the Apostles and their equals. Again, my main point is that our grief and depression may be justly condemned not in themselves but only in respect to their cause and their extent.

When Christ, the light of the world, was led to a cruel death, a number of men and women followed Him, the women bewailing His tragic situation. It was a natural compassion that caused them, when they saw His undeserved misery, to pour forth their tears. Nor was this reproved. But our Lord did remind them gently that in their eagerness to lament, where their tears were not much needed, they had been blind to greater needs for their lamentations. 'Daughters of Jerusalem, weep not for me; weep for yourselves and for your children.'[5]

It is not true, as the Stoics said, that it is unseemly for a wise man to be touched with grief of mind, but it is unwise to be sorrowful without cause – to lament when we should rejoice. To do so demonstrates a lack of wisdom. Again, when the Prophet David says in the 73rd Psalm, 'I have grieved to see the great prosperity of godless men who flourish and go unpunished,' he reveals both his and our mistake in grieving over a situation like this. We err when we grieve at a wicked person's pride and prosperity because seen rightly they neither prosper nor go unpunished.

— *The Folly of Pride* —

It may seem a paradox but it is true that no wicked person's condition is really prosperous, fortunate, or happy. So what if they bless themselves and think they are very happy? Have not demented persons often a high opinion of their own wisdom? It may be that others think of them as they think of themselves. But what others are these? Surely people just like them. Truth and reason view them very differently.

When the Jews wished people prosperity they used a word that means peace. The word prosperity contained within it the meaning of the word peace. When the Prophet plainly said that 'the wicked have no peace', how can we think that they would ever have anything but a vainly imagined happiness?

What wise person ever thought fools happy? If the wicked were wise they would cease to be wicked. Their iniquity proving their folly, how can we doubt their misery? They abound in those things which all men desire. But it is a poor happiness to possess such things. A person to whom God has given riches and treasures and honour may lack nothing that he desires; yet God does not give him the power to enjoy what he has. Solomon says that such prosperity is but vanity, a thing of no value. If such things add nothing to one's happiness when they are not used, surely the more riches that wicked people have and use for evil purposes, the more wretched they are. So now we see what we are to make of their supposed prosperity.

Concerning their pride, the same is true. They are more often plagued than we know. The pangs they feel are not always written in their faces. Though 'wickedness is as sugar in their mouths', and sinfulness like an ointment that makes them look cheerful, nevertheless, if their hearts were disclosed perhaps their glittering condition would not be so envied. The voices that have broken out from some of them – 'O that God had given me a heart as senseless as the flint in the rocks' – reveal persons who taste no pleasure, and feel no woe. These and similar speeches are surely tokens of the curse which Zophar in the Book of Job poured upon the head of the impious man: 'He shall suck the gall of asps and the viper's tongue will slay him.'[6]

If this punishment seems light, because it is secretly pronounced, are we to think they go unpunished when no obvious plague is visited on them? The judgements of God do not always follow crimes as thunder the lightning. Sometimes many ages come between the two. When the sun has shone fair upon the Tabernacle for six days we do not know what clouds the seventh day may bring. And when the punishment does come they will pay with a suffering which takes full account (with interest) of all that has been given to them to enjoy. Or if they chance to escape punishment altogether in this world, which they rarely do, what cave will receive them, what mountain or rock will they pray to have fall upon them in that day when the 'heavens shrivel like a scroll and the mountains move like frightened men from their places'?[7] What cave will hide them from the wrath which they will be able neither to abide nor avoid? No man's misery, therefore, is greater than those whose impiety seems most fortunate. There is much more cause for such persons to bewail their own unhappiness than for others to be troubled by their apparently happy and prosperous condition, as if the hand of the Almighty did not or would not touch them.

For these reasons and others like it, 'be not troubled'.

— *Patience* —

Even though the cause of our depression may be just we should not yield to it with too much self-indulgence. The compassionate grief we feel in the face of the misery of others is the least dangerous to us. But even this grief can lead us to forbear certain obligations rather than to act boldly. And as for the grief brought on by our own sufferings, what temptations have not risen from that depression? The great advantage Satan has taken, even from the godly grief of hearty contrition for sins committed against God, we see clearly in the condition of those whose consciences have brought them to the very brink of extreme depression. Whenever such depression occurs it troubles and unsettles the mind.

Therefore, whether we are moved vainly by that which seems harmful and is not, or have just cause for grief because we are pressed by harmful events, our Saviour's teaching is to 'be not troubled', in the first instance, and to be not overly troubled in the second. For although to have no feelings about what concerns us is stupid, nevertheless, since the Author of our salvation was Himself consecrated by affliction, the path by which we are to follow Him is not strewn with rushes but laid with thorns. Be it ever so hard for us, we must learn to suffer patiently, even that which seems impossible to bear, so that in the hour when God calls us to the final trial and turns this place of honey and pleasure wherein we prosper into that gall and bitterness from which our flesh shrinks, nothing will cause us in our troubled souls to rage at, complain about, or resent God. Every heart must be able, with divinely inspired courage, to impress upon itself the lesson: 'Be not troubled.' In those last and greatest conflicts, remember that nothing we suffer will be so sharp and bitter that we cannot benefit from this encouragement: 'Even learn also patience, O my soul.'[8]

When I say patience, I name that virtue which alone has the power to prevent our souls from being overly troubled. This is a virtue most familiar to those who have been chased out of this earthly life in extreme pain. Does it seem superfluous to discover the manner in which the dead ended their lives? The Lord Himself was not reluctant to register in the book of life how His servants ended their days on earth. He descended to their smallest actions such as what food they wanted during their final illness, what they said to their children, family and friends, where they willed their dead carcasses to be laid, how they framed their last wills and testaments, even to the turning of their dead faces to this side or that, the setting of their eyes, the degrees by which their natural heat had departed them, their cries, their groans, their pantings, breathings, last gaspings. He has most solemnly commended all these details to the memory of all generations.

— *Fear, Death and Sin* —

The concern of the living to live and die well should be increased somewhat when they realize that their death will not be folded up in silence but that the ears of many will be familiar with it. When they hear how mercifully God has dealt with others in their hours of final need, in addition to the praise they give God and the joy which they have, or should have, by reason of their communion with the saints, should they not have assurance about their own final days?

Finally, the sound of those comforting words does not so escape the ears of those who live loose and dissolute lives that they don't sometimes wish in their hearts: 'O that we might die the death of the righteous and that our end might be like theirs.'[9]

However, because to spend too many words on this subject would be to strike wounds in the minds I seek to comfort, let me say this, from my personal knowledge, about the gentlewoman recently deceased: 'She lived like a dove and died a lamb.' Among her many virtues, such as hearty devotion to God, tender compassion to the poor, motherly affection to servants, practical kindness to friends, mild and harmless behaviour toward all, I might add two others that are worthy of mention. In these virtues I would wish that her dearest friends of her own sex would be her closest imitators. They are *silence*, except when duty requires speech, and *patience*, even when extreme pain produces anguish. 'Blessed are they who die in the Lord.'[10] Concerning the dead who are saved, let not the hearts of the living be overwrought with grief.

Concerning fear of evils to come in the next life, in the first place it is clear that we are not afraid of all future maladies. Have we not seen how those who are so tender that they shrink at the first threat of a needle prick will 'kiss the sword that pierces their soul in two'?[11] If every evil caused fear, then sin, which is evil, would be feared. But, properly speaking, sin is not feared as such but only in so far as some harm is attached to it. To teach men to avoid sin it was enough for the Apostle to say, 'fly from it'. To make them fear sin, since the word sin alone did not produce fear, he added that sin is like a 'serpent that stings the soul'.[12]

Again, does fear follow when some new or harmful thing confronts us? No, not unless harmful consequences threaten us either with frustration or vexation and only then when we see no way to escape the impending harm. That which we think we can withstand we do not fear; that which we think we cannot defer or diminish or in any way avoid, we cease to fear and give ourselves over to it. The evil which we fear must be, in our minds, something we are unable to resist, yet is not utterly unavoidable for at least a while. Neither are we very fearful of such threats unless we perceive them to be imminent and near at hand.

Once we have formed an opinion that there are evils that are harmful to our very being and that they are ready to attack us, we feel within us a kind of abhorrence. Because they are near but not yet present, we try to find some way to shift out of their way and save ourselves. Because they cannot be resisted, we try to shun and avoid them. Hence it is that in her extreme fear the Mother of life contracted herself to avoid, so far as she could, the reach of evil and drew into herself the heat and the spirits of the body, leaving the outer parts cold, pale, weak, feeble, and unable to perform the functions of life. We see this in the fear of Balthasar, King of Babel.[13]

From this we see that fear is nothing but a disturbance of the mind caused by an opinion of some imminent evil that threatens to destroy or seriously impair us. If we shun this apparent evil, it contracts and shrinks.

Because here and elsewhere this advice to 'fear not' is often repeated, there are those who pose the tedious question of whether a person may fear destruction without sinning. First, there is that reproof with which Christ rebuked His disciples more than once: 'O men of little faith, why are you afraid?' Second, there is the punishment threatened in the 21st Chapter of Revelation, to wit, 'the lake, the fire and brimstone is not only for murderers, unclean persons, sorcerers, idolaters, liars, but also for the fearful and faint-hearted'. This would seem to argue that fearfulness is a sin.[14]

On the other hand, we observe that a person who has never had even a tendency to sin has still known fear. From this it follows that fear in itself is not sinful. Isn't fear really something natural and necessary for our preservation, something implanted in us by the provident and gracious giver of all good things so that we would not run headlong into harm but have the remedy of avoiding evils which we cannot withstand?

Let those who benefit from the long reign of their princes, let that father or mother who rejoices to see their offspring grow like green and pleasant plants, let those children who would have their parents (and those people who would have their friends) live long lives on this earth (as all people would naturally be happy to do), let them all bless the Father of Lights for giving us fearful hearts which are a protection from many causes of death. Fear, then, being but a part of our nature, cannot in itself be sinful, for sin is not natural but a deprivation of nature.

Still, there are two ways in which, through fear, we can sin. Those are in greatest danger who have no fear of danger. Is there any condition more fearful than that of the Babylonian strumpets who sat on top of the Seven Hills exulting and bragging, 'I am a queen . . .'? How much better and happier are those who speak humbly in this way, 'Lord, from my youth I have borne your burden.'[15]

They who sit in continual ease and are settled into their secure ways, look upon them, look at their faces, listen to their speech, and observe their gestures and their deeds. 'Put them in fear, O God,' says the Prophet, 'so that they may know themselves to be but men,' worms of the earth, 'dust and ashes', frail, corruptible, feeble things. To shake off our false security and breed some healthy fear in the hearts of mortal men there are many admonitions about the power of evil, many threatenings of calamity, many descriptions of what is threatened. These are so lively that they leave an impression deep enough to keep our hearts continually awake.[16]

All of which demonstrates that we should fear nothing so much as the extremity of not being afraid.

— *Fear and Faith* —

When fear has delivered us from that pit wherein those are put who have postponed their judgement days and have made a pact with death by saying, 'Tush, no harm will come to us,' we must take care not to be cast into that place where souls destitute of all hope are plunged. To give ourselves some sense of direction so that we may avoid both of these extremes and be like a ship's captain who knows by his reckoning how much room there is to spare on either side, we must remember that in us Christians there is first our human nature, secondly, the corruption of nature through sin, thirdly, the grace of God which amends and corrects our corruption. Fear operates within all three of these conditions.

Our human nature teaches us to seek our preservation and avoid things we dread. For this reason our Saviour Himself often prayed: 'Father, if it be possible . . .' Our corrupted natures are warned not to stick at things in our temporal affairs which exclude the divine. If it were not for warnings of this kind administered by grace and faith, small evils would soon overwhelm even the best of us. 'A wise man', said Solomon, 'sees the plague coming and hides himself.'[17]

It is nature that teaches the wise man to be fearful and hide himself; but it is grace and faith that teach him where to hide. Fools don't care where they hide their heads. But where shall the wise man hide himself when he fears the plague is coming? Where else should the frightened child hide but in the bosom of his loving father? Where should a Christian hide but 'under the shadow of the wings of Christ his Saviour'?[18]

'Come my people,' says God in Isaiah's prophecy, 'enter into your house, hide yourself . . .'[19] Because we are in danger like pursued birds or like doves that seek but cannot find the resting places that are right in front of them, our Saviour has given us assurance so that fear would never overwhelm us and so that we would remember that, whatever evils may at any time beset us, we can always repair to Him for comfort, counsel and help. For assurance thereof, His 'peace he gave' us, [. . .] not 'such peace as the world offers [. . .] but peace which surpasses all understanding', brings with it complete happiness and continues for ever and ever.[20]

This peace may God the Father grant to you, for his Son's sake, to whom with the Holy Ghost, three persons, one eternal God, be all honour, glory and praise now and for ever.

Amen.

NOTES

1. Philip B. Secor, *Richard Hooker Prophet of Anglicanism* (Burns & Oates, Tunbridge Wells; The Anglican Book Centre, Toronto, 1999), chapters 16, 17, esp. p. 309.
2. W. Speed Hill, gen. ed., *The Folger Library Edition of the Works of Richard Hooker* Vols I–V (The Belknap Press of Harvard University, Cambridge, MA and London, 1977–1990), V, 363–5.
3. Hooker's word for what later came to be called depression is 'heaviness' of spirit, mind or heart.
4. John 12.30; 16.28; 15.11; 14.18; Matthew 28.20; John 14.4; 14.27–28.
5. Luke 23.28.
6. Zophar is the 'impious man' in Job 20.16.
7. Revelation 6.14.
8. Luke 21.19.
9. Numbers 23.10.
10. Revelation 14.13.
11. Luke 2.35.
12. Ecclesiasticus 21.2; 1 Corinthians 15.55–56; Matthew 3.7; 10.23; Luke 3.7; 21.21.
13. Daniel 5—6.
14. Matthew 8.26; Revelation 21.8.
15. Revelation 18.7; Lamentations 3.27.
16. Psalms 9.20; Job 25.6; Psalms 22.6; Genesis 3.19; 18.27.
17. Proverbs 22.3.
18. Psalms 91.4; 17.8.
19. Isaiah 26.20.
20. John 14.27; Philippians 4.7.

— 6 —
Pride

Here we see Hooker probing the nature of human behaviour. Self-understanding is a prerequisite for accepting God's grace. What is there about us that keeps us apart from God? Why do we sin so easily? What can we do to reach beyond and through our human frailty and receive God's love?

This sermon, commonly called 'A Learned Sermon on the Nature of Pride,' is one of three using the prophet Habakkuk for a text. The other two may be dated to 1585 during Hooker's first full year at the Temple Church in London. We may assume that this piece, which is itself composed of more than one sermon, is a part of that series and thus part of Hooker's historic debate with Walter Travers. I have presented here only the first complete segment of the Sermon on Pride. The rest appears in chapter 7 under the title, 'Justice'. I have used Hooker's autograph copy, as transcribed in the Folger Library Edition. [1]

His mind swells and is not right in him; but the just, by faith shall live. Habakkuk 2.4

The nature of man being much more delighted to be led than pulled, he stubbornly resists authority many times over, while to persuasion he yields easily. Thus, the wisest lawmakers have always endeavoured to make those laws seem most reasonable which they most wanted to have inviolably obeyed. A simple law commanding or forbidding is but dead compared to one which expresses the reasons why it commands or forbids. And surely, even concerning the laws of God, although His commandment is in itself reason enough to exact total obedience at the hands of men, there is a strong inducement to obey with greater alacrity and cheerfulness of mind when we see plainly that nothing is imposed to which we must yield unless we are being unreasonable. In a word, whatever we are taught, be it a precept for direction of our manners, or articles for instruction of our faith, or a document which is in any way intended to inform our minds, it takes root and abides in us when we conceive not only what God has spoken, but why.

Furthermore, it is no small matter when we disparage the honour of God's truth, and the comfort, joy and delight we derive from it, by loosely sliding over His speech as though it were vulgar and trivial. For He utters nothing except what delivers substance of doctrine and depth of wisdom in the very choice and framing of His words. His reasoning, however, may not be perceived without a greater exercise of our minds than our little brains are, for the most part, used to. We are reluctant to bring the whole world within our understanding once we have decided that it was only a useless curiosity that led us to delve further than our present wit enabled us to reach.

If I followed this course of reasoning, I might simply tell you that in the first part of His sentence in Habakkuk, God condemns the Babylonian's pride,[2] and in the second part He teaches what will result for the righteous by the constancy of their faith, regardless of the troubles they were suffering. And then, I could simply pass over the rest of my sermon notes, carefully prepared for your instruction as to the meaning of this text, without bothering your minds with any further idle speculation of mine.

But I take it there is a difference between a talk that suits nursing children and their nurses and that by which persons of capacity do – or should – receive instruction.

Based on his earlier discussion of the same subject, Habakkuk, at this point, gives us only a short abridgement of what is later more fully disclosed. Since the question in dispute concerns two sorts of people, the wicked who flourish like the bayleaf and the righteous who are as withered grass – the one sort full of pride and the other cast down with utter discouragement – God seeks to resolve our doubts about both sorts of persons. The sentence from the Prophet, therefore, contains a summary of both the fearful prospects for those who exalt their iniquity and the hope in store for the righteous who are oppressed.

— *Free Will* —

Let us begin by examining what God means in the first part of the statement by the righteousness which He sees lacking in the mind of the Babylonian. All rational beings which God created He made true, good and right: true, in respect to their correspondence to that pattern of their being which was eternally formed in God's foreknowledge; good in regard to the use and benefit which each being gives to each other being; right by an appropriate conformity of all parts of a being with the purpose for which it was intended.

Other, non-thinking, things also have purposes for which they exist. But they lack the faculty to know, judge or treasure these purposes and thus they achieve them unwittingly. Similarly, the means they use to achieve their appointed ends are predetermined and so they cannot turn away from them. For example, the purpose for which the heavens move, the heavens themselves know not; nor can they help but continue their motions. Only humans, in all their actions, know what it is they seek and are not bound by any predetermined means to achieve those ends. In the whole world, no creature but man has the ultimate purpose of his actions held out for him as a recompense and reward. If his mind chooses that purpose, he is thought to have a right or straight mind; if not, his mind is called perverse.

To make this plainer, we note that even as they who travel from city to city inquire for the route that will carry them most quickly to their journey's end, so we, having (as the Apostle says) 'no abiding city',[3] but being always en route to that place of joy, immortality and rest, cannot help in all our deeds, words and thoughts but think that the best route for us is the one that leads most expeditiously to our destination. That route is called 'right thinking'. Even the most desperate despiser of God and godly living seeks the route which leads to that sovereign Good which is the eternal fruition of all goodness and the chief happiness of all human beings.

The difference between right and crooked minds is in the means they follow and avoid in pursuit of their goals. Certain it is that all things which are naturally desired in this world, such as food, clothes, honour, wealth, pleasure and knowledge are subordinated to that future good which we look for in the world to come. Indeed, we pursue these other goals in such a way as we think will lead us to this higher end. Otherwise, we would have to think that when God made promises of good things in this life, He was seeking to pervert us and lead us away from right thinking.

How, then, does the mind of man go astray? His mind is perverse and crooked not when it bends itself toward any of these worldly ends, but when it swerves too far either to the right hand or to the left by giving itself over to excesses or to outright defection from the fundamental rule whereby all human actions are judged. That rule, which measures and judges us, is the law of God. That is why the Prophet makes so frequent and earnest an appeal when he says: 'O, direct me in the ways of thy commandments.'[4] Under the name of this law we must comprehend not only what God has written in tablets and scrolls, but also that which nature has engraved in the hearts of men. Otherwise, how could those heathen who never had books to look upon except the book of nature – the heavens and the earth – be convicted of any perversity?

We see, then, that the heart of a person is not right in any particular unless it is so right in all parts that, when God examines it and calls it to account with all severity and rigour, He is unable to charge it with falling or swerving in any way. When has God ever found such absolute perfection in mere mortals?

Does it not follow that all flesh must, of necessity, fall down and confess: 'We are not dust and ashes, but worse; our minds from the highest to the lowest are not right'? And, if our minds are not right, then undoubtedly they are incapable of that blessedness which, by nature, we seek. Our minds are subject to that which we most abhor: anguish, tribulation, death, woe, endless misery. For whatever misses the mark of the true life will end in perdition. Since everyone is wrapped up in sin and made thereby the child of death, the minds of all being plainly judged not right, shall we then think that God endued His creatures with so many excellent qualities only to leave them in such a state that they could never be happier than if they had never existed?

— *Faith and Works* —

Now there comes, of necessity, a new way to salvation, so that they who were in the perverse mode may be found to be straight and righteous. The old perverse way is the way of nature; the new way is the way of grace. The fulfilment of the first way is salvation earned, presupposing the righteousness of our works, a righteousness grounded in the natural inclination to do good works which God implanted in us. But the way of salvation bestowed upon us by God as a gift does not presuppose our righteousness but the forgiveness of our unrighteousness – which may be called 'justification'.

Justification is not based on our natural inclination to do good, but in our hearty sorrow for not doing so and our sincere belief in Him for whose sake we are accepted. This is our vocation and calling, our 'election' by God who takes us out from the host of His lost children. Christ is the mediator through whose inexplicable and mysterious mercy we are thus saved.

The lack of a clear distinction between these two ways of salvation, and an observation of what they have in common and what is unique to each, has been the cause of most of the confusion under which Christianity labours in our day. The lack of diligence in seeking, setting forth, and exposing the hidden grounds of reason on which the details of each are firmly and strongly built is the cause for all the scruples and doubts that so entangle us and cause so many to despair at ever discerning what is right and what is wrong in anything.

But we will let this matter rest awhile while we search out a reason why some minds may be, and are, truly right, even in the sight of God, although they are in themselves not right.

Now there is this difference between the just and impious: that the mind of one is right in God's sight because his error is not ascribed to him by God, and the other is perverse because his sin is unrepented. However, even as lines may be drawn with a trembling hand and yet, though ragged and uneven, nevertheless point in the right direction compared to those whose lines run clean, but in the wrong direction, so there is no incongruity in terming right-minded those who, though God may charge them with many errors, yet are not like the distorted and ugly monsters who wilfully oppose God. Such men as these have a greater deformity in that they do not understand whether salvation is earned or is freely given by God.

As St Peter said, what is most perverse is when 'the heart is not right in the sight of God.' Thus, regardless of the position one takes on the means of salvation, the orderly disposition of his mind should be such that perturbations and sensual appetites are all kept in check by a moderate and sober will; that the will must be, in all things, controlled by reason; and that reason must be directed by the laws of God and nature.

— *The Roots and Signs of Pride: Ignorance, Vanity, Greed, Arrogance* —

The Babylonian to whom Habakkuk spoke had his mind, as it were, turned upside down. In him, unreasonable wilfulness and blindness trampled all the laws of God and nature underfoot. Wilfulness tyrannized reason and brutish sensuality controlled the will – an evident token that his outrage would work his overthrow and procure his speedy ruin. The origin of his fall is expressed in the prophet's words: 'His mind doth swell.'

Immoderate swelling of the mind is a sign of imminent breach and inevitable destruction – *pride*. Pride is a vice which attaches itself so firmly to the hearts of men that if we were to strip ourselves of all faults one by one, we would without doubt find pride the last and the hardest one to cast off.

I am not talking here merely about that secret itching ailment called vanity with which all persons are affected. The swelling pride of the Babylonian is a thing more meanly inordinate than that. So that we may better conceive of and more easily benefit from an understanding of this vice which sets the whole world off its course and drives so many of even the wisest men beside themselves, we need first of all to explore the nature of pride. Secondly, we will need to uncover the dangers which result from not curing this ill. Lastly, we must find the ways to cure it.

When we look upon the gifts of nature, or of grace, or upon whatever is admired in the world as helpful in adorning our bodies, beautifying our minds or in any way commending ourselves to the judgement or opinion of others, we find that in each case there are some qualities that no one else, or few others, possess. This inequality produces disparagement of people, one by another. This, in turn, produces a sense of pride, born of ignorance. Although men are not proud of anything that is not valued by public opinion, neither are they proud of anything thus valued unless these are possessed by few and desired by all. Only such scarce qualities as these, men believe, will bring honour on those who have them.

Now there is no one so void of brain as to suppose that pride consists in the mere possession of valued and scarce things. For then, to have virtue would be a vice and those would be the happiest who are in fact the most wretched because they have the least of what they desire. Although in our everyday speech we intimate a kind of vanity to be in those favoured by God when we say, 'They are wise men and they know it,'[5] yet this does not prove that every wise man is proud who does not think himself a blockhead. Must we say that when we have something good and know that we have it we give offence by taking joy and delight in it?

What difference is there between men enriched with all abundance of earthly and heavenly blessings and idols that are gorgeously attired but this: the one takes pleasure in what he has and the other does not. If we may be possessed of beauty, strength, riches, power, knowledge; if we are in every way glad and joyful for our own welfare, and in all this remain unblameable, still, there are some who, granting all this, doubt if it is consistent with proper humility to accept testimonies of praise and commendation, titles, houses, and other honours which the world gives as acknowledgement of some men's excellence above others. But Christ said to His own, 'The kings of the gentiles reign over them [. . .] and are called gracious lords. But it is not so with you.' On the other hand, the Anabaptists urge equality amongst all Christians as if all exercise of authority were nothing more than heathenish pride.[6]

Our Lord and Saviour had no such meaning. His disciples, feeding themselves with a vain imagination of the day when as Messiah of all the world He would erect His throne in Jerusalem, and exercise dominion with great pomp and stateliness, higher than all the princes of the earth, began to think how their own status would rise along with their Lord's. Since they had left behind and forsaken everything to follow Him, their place in His circle should not be small. Because there were many of them, they were troubled about which would be the greatest. Two of them made suit to the Lord that one should sit at His right hand and the other at His left. The others began to bellow, each taking offence that any one should have what all of them desired.

To correct this ill humour, their Lord and master turned aside their thoughts from such vain and fanciful conceits and gave them to understand plainly that they were deceiving themselves. He had come not to purchase an earthly kingdom but to bestow a heavenly kingdom within which the greatest would be those whose unabashed humility made them, in this world, the lowest and least among all others. My kingdom, He told them, is not such as you dream of. Therefore, these hungry contentions among you are more fitting in heathens than in you.

Nothing was farther removed from Christ's intention than that there should be these distinctions in titles and callings annexed for the sake of rankings to either ecclesiastical or civil authority. But when we examine thoroughly the nature of vice, no one will be so simple-minded as not to see that there can be an uglier posture, many times over, in rejecting honours offered than in trying to exact them from people. As Judas' care for the poor was mere covetousness and as the honest wastefulness spoken of in the Gospel was actually a form of thrift, so there is no doubt that going about in rags can be a form of pride and thrones can, in reality, be an honest humility.

We must, therefore, probe somewhat deeper before we come to the closet wherein this poison, pride, lies. There is, in the heart of every proud person, a vain opinion of his own excellencies that leads to a false understanding that his worthiness of esteem, regard and honour is greater than, in truth, it is. This leads him, in all of his inner attitudes, to raise himself up and to fashion his outward acts accordingly. If you want a list of examples of this behaviour, you may either call to mind those whom God Himself noted in Scripture to have this fault, or you may recall what you observe daily in the odious lives and manners of high-minded people.

It would take too long to gather the plentiful harvest of examples of such evil behaviour in sacred Scripture. That which we drink in with our ears does not so piercingly enter our minds as that which is conveyed by sight. Is there anything written in the tenth chapter of Isaiah concerning the Assyrian monarch with his swelling mind, his haughty looks and his presumptuous pride when he says, 'by the power of my own hand I have done all things and by my own wisdom I have subdued the world'? Is there anything in the third chapter of Isaiah concerning the Dames of Zion, of their 'stretched out necks, their immodest eyes, their pageant-like, stately and pompous gait'? Is there anything there concerning the practices of Core, Dathan and Abiram, of their impatience under a life of subjugation, their mutinous complaining under lawful authority, their grudging against their ecclesiastical and civil superiors? Is there anything about pride in any of the parties and sects in our own day which is not as clear as glass for all to behold?[7]

If books, both profane and holy, were all lost, as long as the manners of men retain the state they are now in, anyone can observe that once these people conceive an overweening impression of themselves, how their desires swell, how deadly their hatred becomes, how heavy their displeasure, how much more unappeasable their indignation and wrath are than other people's. We observe in what manner they compose themselves to be deviants, outside the compass of all rules which measure the common sort, how the oaths which cause the hearts of religious people to tremble are but manners of graceful speech to them.

We also see how happy the proud are to see the enormity of their crimes above the reach of laws and punishments; how much it delights them when they are able to show disdain with the darkness of their looks; how far they exceed the bounds which should limit their attitudes; how high they bear their heads above others; how they intimidate all who do not accept their words as oracles of wisdom with applause and approval; how they look upon others with indirect countenance, listening patiently to nothing except praise of themselves, nor speaking without scornfulness and disdain; how they use their servants as if they were beasts, their inferiors as servants, their equals as inferiors, and, as for their superiors, they acknowledge none.

We notice also how the proud admire themselves as venerable, powerful, wise, circumspect, provident and in every way great, taking all men but themselves to be but ciphers – poor, inglorious, simple creatures, needless burdens, nothings. In a word, for anyone who observes how strange and outlandish these people are in all things, it is not hard to gather that pride is nothing but an inordinate elation of the mind that proceeds from a false conception of a person's excellence in honourable things which, in turn, frames his opinion of all his deeds and behaviour, unless he is cunning enough to conceal it. A foul scar may be covered with a fair cloth. As proud as Lucifer is, he may in outward appearance be lowly.

No one expects to harvest grapes from thistles. Nor from a bad nature can suitable fruits be looked for. Whatsoever harm comes to families because of disobedience of children, stubbornness of servants, intractableness of wives (who though in all other things they may rule are still subject due to the inequality of their sex), or whatever harm comes from strife among people within the fellowship of various communities or from the tyranny of rulers, the ambitions of nobles, the rebellion of subjects, the heresies, schisms, and divisions in the church – in all these situations when we name *pride*, we name the mother that brought them forth and the only nurse that feeds them.

Give me the hearts of all people humbled and what is there that can overthrow and disturb the peace of the world? Although many things are the cause of much evil, pride is the cause of all evil.

— *Remedies to Pride* —

To declaim the swarms of evils issuing from pride is an easy task. I wish I could as exactly prescribe and persuade you of the effective remedies whereby this grievous sore might be cured, the means by which the pride of swelling minds might be reduced. We have already said enough about the cause that breeds pride to be pointed in the right direction for finding the most likely remedy for removing it. Diseases that come from fullness are relieved by emptiness. Pride is not cured except by abating the error that caused the mind to swell.

Seeing that these proud people swell due to a misconception of their own excellence, anything that tends to beat down their pride, whether it be pronouncements from other people or chastisements from God Himself, will make them cease to be proud, so long as they cause them to see the error of overvaluing the thing of which they are proud. This was the aim of Job in his response to his eloquent friends. Perceiving how much they delighted in hearing themselves talk, as though they were giving their poor afflicted friend a schooling of marvellous, deep and rare instruction, as if they had taught him more than all the world could ever acquaint him with, Job's response was to this effect: 'You swell up as though you had conceived some great truth but who does not already know everything that you are setting forth? Is any man really ignorant of these things of which you speak?'

— *False Humility* —

Do not boast. What have you and what are you, in and of yourselves? All those humble confessions of yours have been forever in the mouths of the Saints who have truly waded into their own sinfulness. As the Prophet said, 'We are nothing but sores and festering corruption.'[8] Our very light is darkness, our righteousness is corruption. As St Gregory said, 'Let no man ever put confidence in his own accomplishments. In the sight of that Dreadful Judge, what seems such a beautiful show at the doors of judgement is but so much noise.' And recall St Anselm's words: 'I adore Thee. I shall bless the Lord God of heaven and the Redeemer of the world with all the power, ability and strength of my heart and soul. For your goodness is so immeasurably extended, without regard for my merit, for which only torments would be due if it were not for Your mercy.'[9]

If all these reverend Fathers whose books are so full of sentences witnessing their own Christian humility were raised from the dead and could behold with their own eyes what they have written, would they not pronounce themselves fuller of Lucifer than of Christ, because they were proud-hearted men with minds more swelling with pride than a sincere and feeling Christian can tolerate?

Even as unruly children with whom wholesome admonition yields little response are brought to fear for ever that which they have been well whipped for doing, so the mind which does not yield to instruction will cease to swell under the rod of divine punishment. If, therefore, the prophet Daniel, instructed by good experience, acknowledged that God's rod reformed him [. . .] and if the blessed Apostle Paul needed 'the corrosive pain of sharp and bitter strokes lest his heart should swell with too great an abundance of heavenly revelation', surely whatever God inflicts upon us in this world is not more than our pride requires, for the sake of both punishment and reformation.[10]

So hard it is to cure a sickness like pride because the very remedies that cure other vices cause this one. If we were clean from all spots and blemishes, including pride itself, we might still be proud that we were not proud. Thus it is often God's wisdom to suffer a just person to fall so that being raised up again he might learn what power it was that upheld him. I am not afraid to affirm boldly, with St Augustine, that people who are puffed up with a proud opinion of their own righteousness and holiness may actually benefit when God, in his grace, permits them to sin grievously. By this means their excessive liking of themselves may be supplanted with a more realistic dislike of themselves.[11] Ask the very soul of Peter and undoubtedly he will answer you to the effect that his eager protestations of faith, made in the glory of his strength, he is now ashamed of. But those crystal tears bewailing his sin and weakness have procured his endless joy. His strength has been his ruin and his fall has been his salvation.[12]

We will recall, once more, Habakkuk's two complaints to God on behalf of God's afflicted people: firstly, that the impious and cruel persecutors of men flourish; secondly, that the saints are persecuted by such cruelty and must suffer such a woeful and hard condition. We now see that the swelling pride of the persecutors foretells their speedy ruin, whereas those who counted themselves the children of death may hope for a new life that will cause their bruised hearts to rejoice. [. . .] They may now put off sackcloth and change their doleful tunes into songs of cheerful melody. They may shake off their deep depression and resume their joy – a joy born of their faith in the promise of new life, as foretold in the words of Second Corinthians 6.9, 'Like dead men yet behold, alive.' For 'the just man shall live by his faith'. These words lead us to speak first of the promise of new life, secondly of the quality of those to whom the promise is made, and, lastly, of the extent to which the lives of the justified may be said to depend upon their faith.[13]

In nature, those things are said to live which are motivated by a power within them which gives them motion. They have motion for as long as they are said to have life. They are not moved by any external force but by a certain divine vigour which nature has breathed into them. Human beings, of all living creatures the most important, have that life which the soul within them causes. Some of them have a spiritual quality wrought by a special divine power inhabiting their souls. Now we should consider first the original source of spiritual life, then the manner in which we are now living the life of God, and thirdly how this spiritual life may be perfected in the world to come.

'I have set before you', said Moses, 'life and death. Choose life so that both you and your descendants may live by loving the Lord your God, by obeying his voice and by cleaving to him. For he only is your life and the length of thy days.' [. . .] Similarly, the Apostle John writes, 'As the father has life in himself, so to the Son he has given life, from himself, also.' This gift of life to the Son was so that others might be made alive from his quickening force and virtue. The Apostle Peter calls Christ 'the life of the world' partly because He suffered death to procure eternal life for others and partly because the world itself was revivified by His death.[14]

Unless Christ is truly in you, you cannot be made alive through His life. Many apostolic and evangelical sentences testify to this truth. Paul in the eighth chapter of Romans says, 'If Christ is in you, then the body is dead unto sin but the spirit lives for the sake of righteousness'; in the second chapter of Galatians, 'Christ Jesus lives in me'; in the third chapter of Ephesians, 'For this cause I bow my knees to the Father of our Lord Jesus Christ, that he may grant you, according to the riches of his glory, to be strengthened in the inner man so that Christ may dwell in your hearts'; in St John we read, 'He that is within you is greater than he who is in the world.'[15]

It seems somewhat strange that something so often expressed in Scripture should be so poorly understood. It is generally agreed that 'he who has not the Son of God within him has not life'.[16] We must learn how to understand this. Some think this truth is an inexplicable mystery which everyone must believe but no one will ever understand. Others, believing that if we could never understand the meaning of God's words then we might as well call them frivolous and vain, have expounded a theory in which our conjunction with Christ is a mutual participation whereby we and He are blended with each other, His flesh and blood with ours and ours with His, as materially as wax melts and blends into one lump.

This gross idea flies in the face of reason. Are not we and Christ distinct personalities? Are we not physically divided and severed from one another? When the Apostle wrote, 'My little children, of whom I travail in birth again until Christ be formed in you', did he mean materially and actually to create Christ in them, flesh and blood, body and soul?[17] No. As Gregory Nazianzus said, 'Christ is in us [not] according to that natural substance which is visibly seen on earth but according to that intellectual comprehension which the mind is capable of.' So, the difference between Christ on earth and Christ in us is no less than that between a ship on the sea and in the mind of him that built it: the one a sensible thing, the other the mere concept of a sensible thing. The way in which the Apostle gave form to Christ was in the Gospel. Christ was formed, therefore, when Christianity was created and comprehended.[18]

All things which we know and delight in dwell in our minds and possess our hearts. Thus Christ, knowing His sheep and being known by them – loving and being loved – may properly be said to be in them, and they in Him. And since we are not capable of this comprehension on our own, God has given to us His Spirit to teach us to acknowledge in our hearts and confess with our tongues that Christ is the Son of the living God.

Concerning the source and fountain of life, I have said enough.

— *New Life in Christ* —

Concerning the matter of the status of spiritual life here on earth, we notice that among those who walk in the blind vanity of their own minds, who have darkened their thoughts with ignorance and hardened their hearts to the point that they are without consciences, who have given themselves over to wantonness, who are greedily set upon by all uncleanness and sin, it is clear that they are dead. They are strangers to the life of God – a life which is nothing else but a spiritual and divine kind of being which we attain by a rebirth in which Christ and His spirit dwell within us. Thus the Soul within our souls moves us to inner attitudes and outward actions that are acceptable in the sight of God.

As people who, living out their natural lives, are nourished by nature, so the person to whom the Spirit of Christ gives life also delights in His spiritual food. He 'hungers after righteousness'. It is meat and drink for him to be exercised in doing good works.

[. . .] What delights the senses of those who live the life of God is suggested by the words of Solomon when he says that for taste let it be that 'honey and milk are under their tongue', for smell, let it be 'a bundle of myrrh or a cluster of camphor', for hearing, 'O let me hear thy voice, thy voice delectable', for seeing, 'show me thy countenance, thy sight is comely'.[19]

Even as with the senses, so the motions of the person who lives the life of God have a special excellence. His hands are not stretched toward his enemies except to give them alms. His feet are slow except when he is travelling for the benefit of his brothers and sisters. When he is railed upon by wicked persons, he replies with the words of Stephen: 'Lord, lay not this thing to their charge.'[20] If we could live three times as long as Methuselah, or live as long as the moon will endure, what would our natural life amount to without this new life in Christ? This new life alters our corrupt nature. By this we are continually stirred up to do good things; by this we are led to abhor the gross defilements of this wicked world, yet constantly and patiently to suffer whatever befalls us as though 'as sheep we are led by flocks unto the slaughter'.[21]

This new life in us dispels the clouds of darkness, eases the grief in our hearts, abates hatred, eases strife, appeases anger, orders our emotions, governs our thoughts, guides our lives and our conversations. Where do we find such innocence as in Abel, such piety as in Enoch, such equity as in Noah, such faith as in Abraham, such simplicity as in Isaac, such long suffering as in Jacob, such chastity as in Joseph, such meekness and tenderness as in the heart of Moses, such devotion as in Samuel, such humility as in Daniel, such authority as in Elias, such zeal as in Elizeus, such courage as in the prophets, such love as in the Apostles, such patience as in the Martyrs, such integrity as in all the Saints? And did they not all live the life of God?

The life in God begun here will be finished in the world to come. And, when we have spoken all we can say, it comes to this: the person who has the life of God has more than words can possibly express, more than his heart can desire; he is full and has enough. For the words of the promise of life in the tenth chapter of John are clear: 'I came that my sheep might have life and have it abundantly.'

Seeing that we are taught that God's life in us is our inheritance and that when we have it we have enough, why do we struggle so much for other things that are all around us and that we crave? When we leave this world the hope of full life in God does not leave us, not even in the grave of death. The casualties of this present world are various. The trials we are subject to are many and fearful. But in the midst of all this, the major anchor for our souls is this: *the just shall live*. God sets this promise before the eyes of His poor and afflicted people as having sufficient force to countervail whatever misery they have or might yet sustain. These dreadful fears of troubles, wars, and invasions, the very mention of which so terrifies us and weighs down our hearts, are dissolved in this promise: *the just shall live*.[22]

And what are these fears of ours but panicky terrors? If those who promise great things have no power to perform them even in the least degree, what wise person is there among you who is not moved to laugh at such presumptuous promises? Yet, behold how at the mere threatenings of men we tremble even though we know that their rage is hollow and they cannot do what they intend, and even though we know that God has numbered the hairs on our heads and not even one of them will fall to the ground without the consent of our heavenly Father.

How often has God turned aside attempts to bring death to his Saints and instead saved their lives and increased their honours? Was it not so with Joseph, Moses, David and Daniel? Even if cruelty, oppression and tyranny have so far advanced that their objectives are satisfied and they prosper by what they seize, the utmost that such evils can do is but the good which the blessed Apostle desired all along. *Cupio dissolvi*.[23] Thrice happy, therefore, are those who, whatever misery may befall them in this world, are secure in a certain expectation of what God has promised: happiness and true life in the world to come. Of this life, God the Father makes you partakers through the merits of His only begotten Son, our blessed

Saviour, unto whom, with the Holy Ghost, three persons – one, eternal and ever-living God – be honour, glory and praise for ever.

Notes

1. For a discussion of the provenance of this tractate see W. Speed Hill, gen. ed., *The Folger Library Edition of the Works of Richard Hooker* Vols I–V (The Belknap Press of Harvard University, Cambridge, MA and London, 1977–1990), V, 299–308.
2. Although 'Babylon' was, in Hooker's day, a metaphor for the Roman Church and 'Babylonians' often referred to the Pope and his bishops, Hooker uses the word here as Habakkuk did: to refer to the captors of the ancient Jews.
3. Hebrews 13.14.
4. Psalms 119.35.
5. Ecclesiastes 8.1, 5; Job 37.24; Proverbs 26.12; 28.11.
6. Luke 22.25–26. Anabaptists in Hooker's day urged an egalitarian church polity and, in the opinion of some of their enemies, they opposed all civil government as well. See *Folger Edition*, V, 807.
7. Isaiah 10.13; 3.16; Numbers 16.1–3. Core, Dathan and Abiram rebelled against Moses and Aaron.
8. Isaiah 1.6.
9. Gregory I, *Expositio*, 5.7. St Anselm (1033–1109) was Archbishop of Canterbury and a leading medieval theologian. Hooker's source here is unknown.
10. Psalms 119.67, 71; 2 Corinthians 12.7.
11. St Augustine, *De Civitate Dei*, 14.13 (*The City of God*, trans. Marcus Dods, The Modern Library, New York, 1950, pp. 460–2).
12. Matthew 26.33–35; Mark 14.29; John 13.37–38; 2 Corinthians 12.9–10.
13. 2 Corinthians 6.9; Hebrew 2.4.
14. Deuteronomy 30.19–20; John 6.26, 63; 1 Corinthians 15.45; Acts 3.15.
15. Romans 8.10; 2 Corinthians 13.15; Ephesians 3.14, 16–17; 1 John 4.4.
16. John 3.36.
17. Galatians 4.19.
18. Gregory Nazianzus (329–389) was an early exponent of the distinction between the phenomenal and the noumenal. For the full citation and for an opinion that Hooker misunderstood (or misused) this source, see *Folger Edition*, V, 812–13.
19. Matthew 5.6; John 4.34; Romans 14.17; Galatians 2.20; Psalms 34.8; Song of Solomon 4.11; 1.12; 2.14.
20. Acts 7.60.
21. Psalms 44.22.
22. Habakkuk 2.4.
23. This is the desire to be 'dissolved' and thus to be with Christ. Philippians 1.23.

— 7 —
Justice

There is no separate sermon in the Hooker canon on the subject of justice. But the second and third portions of the 'Sermon on Pride' so clearly comprise a separate piece on this subject that I have treated them as such here.

Among other topics relevant to the subject of justice, we have here a taste of Hooker's famed discussions, in his Of the Laws of Ecclesiastical Polity, *on the origins and functions of law.*

There never was that person who was so careless about the welfare of his own soul that, knowing about salvation yet living a life of destructive behaviour, he did not harbour a secret and natural desire to live rather than to perish. 'What man is he', asked the prophet David, 'who desires not a life of days wherein he may see everlasting good?'

> Let that man keep his tongue from harm, his lips from guile; let him shun evil, embrace good, pursue peace and follow after it. For the eyes of the Lord are on the righteous and his ears are open to their cry. Their cry he hears and delivers them from all their troubles; he is near to them who are contrite in heart; men afflicted in spirit he will save; the troubles of the righteous are great but he delivers them out of all of them; their very bones are so carefully kept that not as much as one of them is broken; the Lord redeems the souls of his servants and none that trust in him shall perish.'[1]

Whatever we may say about the watchful eye of God, His attentive ear, the nearness of His spiritual assistance when we are in trouble, the promises of salvation, redemption, safe preservation of our souls and bodies and our very bones, the promise of life includes them all. All these various particular aspects: harmlessness and sincerity in speech, adverseness to evil, inclinations to good things, pursuit of peace, humility of spirit, integrity, obedience, trust in God, what do they all mean but what is meant by the word justice? Justice expresses fully the quality of those to whom God promises life.

To touch lightly on a matter of such importance as justice is itself an offence to justice. I would not let pass such a fit occasion to wade into this subject further than might be expedient were not the weight and import of the issue so urgent.

Justice is that which, when it flourishes upholds, and when it does not prevail, its opposite shakes and threatens with utter desolation and ruin, the whole world. Justice is that whereby the poor have their help, the rich their ease, the powerful their honour, the souls of the departed their endless rest and quietness. Justice is that by which God and angels and men are principally exalted. Justice is the chief matter in contention today in the Christian world. In a word, justice is that wherein not only our present happiness but our future joy in the kingdom of God depends. Whether we are in love with the one or the other, with things present or to come, we need to be instructed in justice. In that study the first thing to be examined is the nature of justice in general; the second, justice which is in God; lastly, that justice whereby we ourselves may expect the life that is promised to us in the words of the prophet, when he said, 'By faith they shall live.' [2]

God created nothing simply for itself. But each thing has such an interest in all things, and each part in every part, that in the whole world nothing is found wherein one part thereof can say, 'I don't need you.' To express this truth, the prophet Hosea developed a delightful metaphor in which the people of Israel are suitors of corn, wine and oil, as if these were men of power who could do them a good turn. The corn, wine and oil are supplicants to the earth; the earth to the heavens, the heavens to God. 'In that day,' says the Lord, 'I will hear the heavens and the heavens shall hear the earth, and the earth shall hear the corn, wine and oil; and the corn, wine and oil shall hear Israel.' They are said to hear that for which they ask, and to ask for what they need to have.[3]

Our Lord, the supreme commander arranged it so that each creature should have some particular task and charge which goes beyond its own preservation. The sun does us well by giving heat and light, the moon and stars by their secret influences, the air and wind by every one of their many qualities, the earth by receiving all of these and transmitting them to her inhabitants. How beneficial by their very nature are the operations of all things. We are unable to grasp fully the extent of these benefits in part because of God's incomprehensible greatness, in part because of our own inattention and carelessness.

Because the evidence is right in front of us, we cannot ignore the fact that whatever in nature excels in pre-eminence and honour is of greatest value and benefit to other things. This fact should be an inducement to God's children to delight in imparting to others the good that has been bestowed upon them in proportion to what they have received. The good things in life are known to be communicable by those who possess them; they are known to be derived from others and to be transferable to those in need of them. In these transactions lies the exercise of justice.

These good things of which I speak are of two kinds: they are either good and desirable to the person who receives them, such as counsel in perplexity, help in need, comfort in sorrow and grief. Although not desired in themselves, they are valuable in the furtherance of some larger good. For example, punishments that are much feared by those who may suffer from them are necessary to ensure the public welfare.

Now, since God has so furnished the world that there is nothing we need that cannot be obtained, justice is that virtue whereby the good which we lack is received, inoffensively, from the hands of others. I say inoffensively, for we must note that, although the need of any person signifies a defect in that mutual assistance which characterizes the exercise of justice, yet merely to have such want supplied is far from the true exercise of equity and justice.

We must find some rule or law that determines what every

person is due, and from whom and how it is to be had. Justice can be defined as that virtue which assures that we have what we need in the manner prescribed by law. Neither God nor angels nor men may in any sense be called just except by reference to some law of justice that operates among them. Such a law may be natural and immutable or else a law, subject to change, which we call 'positive law'. The failure to distinguish between these two types of law has obscured the meaning of justice more than a little.

— *Laws Changeable and Immutable* —

It is no small perplexity that is bred in the minds of many people when they observe that the laws which God has given are abrogated and annulled by human authorities who take it upon themselves to subject God's ordinances to their own devices and imagine that they are wiser than God Himself. When popular discourses to this effect are polished with the art and cunning of which some men are very capable, it is not difficult to enchant the most religiously disposed person with such tunes. The root of this error is a misconception that all laws that men establish are 'positive', and so changeable, and all laws which God establishes are immutable. Not so. It is not the author but the object of a law that defines the distinction. The Roman laws *Hominen indemnatum ne occidito, Patronis si clienti fraudem facerit sacer esto* were unchangeable laws, though made by men.[4] Similarly, all those Jewish ordinances for civil punishment of malefactors: 'The prophet that entices men to idolatry shall be slain; a false witness shall suffer the same hurt which his testimony might have brought upon another, life for life, eye for eye, tooth for tooth.'[5]

On the other hand, all Apostolic canons concerning church government, though received from God Himself, are positive laws and therefore alterable.

They differ in this way: a positive (changeable) law is one that binds those who receive it in those things which might previously have been done or not done without offence. But the rule applies for only so long as the law is in force. Such, for example, were those church laws concerning *strangulation and blood*. On the other hand, there is no person and no time for which an unchangeable law of nature is not binding. If, for example, God had never spoken a word to us concerning the duty which children owe to their parents, yet from the first-born of Adam until the very last of us, *Honour thy father and thy mother* would have bound all of us. For this reason, to dispense with the one sort of law – natural law – can never be just; whereas, it can sometimes be an injustice not to dispense with the other – positive law.

Therefore justice always implies these things: first, that there is some good thing that is due from one person to another; secondly, that there is a law, either natural or positive, that makes this an obligation; thirdly, that the person who has the obligation does what the law commands.

The several kinds of distributive, cumulative and corrective justice I will not talk about on this occasion. But before we begin to speak of God's justice, I will note one general point about justice among men. The singular complaint about justice in the mouths of all people, and not without cause, is: 'There is no justice.'[6]

— *Nature and Cause of Injustice* —

Because all people succumb to such utter despair over ever devising some remedy for the great malady of injustice, we must examine patiently the means to endure the ensuing wrongs and injuries resulting therefrom. Although the cause of injustice is usually general in nature, we are inclined to charge particular persons with this heavy wrong. We should be wary of doing this lest blaming others subjects us to blame. What is more injurious than falsely accusing another of a wrong? It cannot be denied that we can always find reasons to blame one another for injustices done among us. However, patience, contentment and wise, considerate meditation might cut off many of the scandalous accusations that are so often and so grievously poured into the ears of people without regard for what is fair to them or their communities. Perhaps these kindled affections would be better cooled with sober advice than enflamed by encouraging our displeased minds.

No person ever thinks the injuries he receives are small. Yet when we first receive an injury, how do we know any wrong was actually done to us? How do we discern that we have not deserved the injury? Do we not measure what is due us in terms of our own desires? When we lack that which we think we should have, we conclude that we have been wronged. Might not Daniel be thus condemned for being unjust to the Babylonian? The Jews to the Persians? Our Lord Himself to the high priest, Annas, before whom He stood in judgement?

'No man can be a competent judge in his own case.'[7] Therefore, it is rash for us, on our own authority, to say that any person is unjust. If we abated such a practice, many accusations of wrongdoing would be answered before they were made. Once again, we must remember that we should claim nothing on our behalf, or that of others, unless there is warrant for doing so in the law and unless the judgement is handed down by at least two persons other than ourselves.

Do we think it is easy to determine the meaning of the law? I will propose to you one example to show that there is often a great likelihood that what may appear to be equitable in law in fact is not. There was once a law among the Greeks that whoever killed a tyrant could name his own reward and claim it at the hands of the chief magistrate. There was another law that whenever a tyrant was slain his five closest relatives should also be put to death. The tyrant Alexander Phereus was treacherously murdered by his own wife. She then demanded as her reward that her son by Phereus be spared despite the law that required his execution.[8]

The question is whether justice is served by granting or denying her request. On the one hand, all commonwealths depend for their security no less on payment of promised rewards than on taking promised revenge. If we cannot rely on the legal guarantees of such rewards and punishments, who would ever risk such a dangerous undertaking as killing a tyrant? If in this case the law had said that the son of a murdered tyrant need not be executed, that son might remain loyal to his country rather than seek revenge for the deserved murder of his father. Since punishments are, if anything, best lessened and rewards enlarged, what if the son and not the mother in this case had murdered the tyrant? Should his action, though rewardable by law, be punished because he is a close blood relative to his father? It is a hard thing that the father's offence (tyranny) should be a greater disadvantage to the son than his mother's reward. It would undoubtedly inhibit rulers from becoming tyrants if they knew that enmity toward them would always be rewarded.

On the other side of the argument there is as much if not more justice. Whenever two laws, through an unintended result, contradict one another in such a way that both cannot be followed, there is nothing for it but to obey that law which will do the least harm to the public good. In this case it is not hard to see that the law which benefits the common safety (killing the son of a murdered tyrant) is preferable to the law which benefits only one person (saving the life of the son as a reward to the mother who murdered the tyrant). This conclusion is further supported when we consider that fathers are often more careful about their children than themselves. Thus, tyrants, being more afraid of the overthrow of their progeny than of their own welfare, might be even more inclined to be tyrannical if they thought their actions would not impose legal penalties on their children. Also, is it not intolerable that an act so monstrous as a woman murdering her husband not only receives no punishment but actually is rewarded?

Finally, the law requires that any demand for reward for killing a tyrant must be granted. Yet when a particular reward is demanded (the death of the tyrant's next of kin), the very purpose of the other more general law (elimination of tyrants) is abridged. Otherwise the absurd result of these laws would be that the licence to exercise tyranny is required in order that tyrants might be removed.

We conclude that it is not simply what people seek under the law, but what they seek that is reasonable and does not produce contradictions in the law, that is lawful.

This example may be enough to show how hard it is even for the wisest and most skilful among us to discern what is justice and what is not, so much so that to others as well as to ourselves it may seem that we are wronged when we are not. Furthermore, even when we are denied what we by right are entitled to, it may be that those who do us wrong have not injured us in a way that we may rightly call unjust. There is no injustice unless a wrong is wilfully committed. We are unjust when we accuse those who act wrongfully not out of intent but out of habit. When we do not receive what we are entitled to from others, it may actually be contrary to the wills of those who act wrongly towards us. Such persons are to be pitied rather than accused.

Even if persons bend themselves against us intentionally and maliciously, we would do well to abate the keen edge of our indignation by remembering the wrongs that we commit. We don't answer to God for our wrongs even once in a thousand times; but if one of a thousand wrongs done to us by others goes unpunished we are unable to bear the injustice of it.

To conclude on this point: even if we had never injured either God or one another, the patience and meekness of Christ in putting up with injuries done to Him is worthy of our imitation. His humility ought to be sufficient to humble us no matter how grievous and insufferable the wrongs done to us may seem. If, therefore, others are not persuaded to do us justice, let the persuasion of Christ's example induce us to endure wrongs done to us with patience and to show ourselves as truly just persons by bearing the cross which men's injustice lays upon us. May God the Father grant us the wisdom to do so, for the sake of His Son, unto whom, with the Holy Spirit, three persons yet one eternal living God, be honour, glory, and praise for ever.

— *The Reasonableness of God's Justice*[9] —

We have spoken thus far of the nature of justice in general. Now we must address God's justice. Lest anyone should think that I speak of God as just in the sense that our own self-love leads us to think that God must embody our noblest quality, I will need to demonstrate to you that by His very nature God possesses within Him a divine virtue called justice. Secondly, I will show you in what manner God exercises this virtue in the affairs of His creatures; thirdly, what wrong we do to God by failing to understand how He dispenses justice to us; and lastly, what honour is shown God and what benefit we receive from Him by having a true knowledge of His justice.

I would have a large and abundant field to walk through if I tried to collect all the good reasons and convincing arguments available to demonstrate that, as we see in the 33rd chapter of Exodus, God insinuates that He is all good. For in his response to Moses' request to show him His glory, God says, 'I will make all goodness to go before you.'[10] Even as there can be no warmth in any particular thing that is not contained in some universal heat, so, since God is infinite, if we find justice to be any part of God's goodness, then by definition God is just.

Who would not account justice to be more than a small part of the good things of life? For sake of argument, let us make the case that angels and men are just and God is not. Would they not then in this aspect of goodness be better than Him to Whom the title of greatest and best is said to be due? Besides, God Himself being the supreme cause that gives life to all things that exist, and every effect resembling the cause from which it comes, it follows that either we are not made righteous by God or, if we are, then surely God Himself is much more than what He has made. Indeed, He is the author, the fountain, and the cause of our justice.

Finally, seeing that we cannot conceive of God without correspondence between Him and the creatures who receive their nature and their properties from Him, either we must think that God by His very nature cannot help but give good things to His creatures – in which case why should they give Him thanks and worship Him? – or that He distributes His grace advisedly according to some law which tells Him upon whom and why and wherefore He should bestow His goodness. In that case, we might call God just because the nature of justice is to make such decisions. As we have said, justice is that virtue wherein we receive good things in such manner and degree as the law prescribes.

However, this doubt may be raised: since God has no superior and is subject and bound to obey no higher authority and power, there is no one who can lay a law upon Him. How then can there be any justice in His doing what no authority or law can bind Him to do? To this question we could make no answer at all if we held as they do who peremptorily avow that there is no *Why*, i.e., no reason for what God does, except to say that it is His absolute will to do it.

True enough, the Prophet said in the 115th Psalm, 'Our God is in heaven and whatsoever he wills he does.' And our Saviour says in Matthew's Gospel, 'I give thanks O Father in heaven and earth because thou hast hid these things from the wise men and men of understanding and opened them to babes . . .' And the blessed Apostle Paul said, 'God predestined, called, saved, and accomplished all things according to the purpose of his own will.' [11]

What are we to infer from this? That there is no other cause in any of the works of God to be discovered or rendered but this? If so, then it seems that when people asked, in the fifth chapter of Jeremiah, 'Wherefore has our Lord done these things?', God should have closed up their mouths with a sharp reproof for asking such a question. But He commanded the prophet to satisfy their minds by giving some reason for His actions. 'Thou shalt answer them: "Even as you have forsaken me and served strange gods in your land, so shall you also serve strangers in a land that is not yours."' [12] When we sift through these sentences it soon appears that there is no denial here of some reason for the works of God.

Our nature is prone to haughty conceits. When we see blessings abundantly poured upon us which God has withheld from others, we easily imagine that we have more because we are worthier than others are. To pull down this proud opinion it is often impressed upon us that whatever we possess is not owing to our worth but to His mercy, not to our merit, but to His goodness. Yes, even in the very place in Scripture where the blessed Apostle sets forth our predestination and adoption through Christ to be owing to the pleasure of God's will, we are given immediately a reason for God's action, namely, that we would thereby give praise to Him for His grace.

Seeing then that God does nothing except for some purpose and that that purpose is the reason for what He does, may we not conclude that all that God does is according to a rule which prescribes His actions? Is not the purpose of God's actions a law? And does not that law of God strictly require that all His actions are as they are in the sense that if they were any different they would not conform to their appointed purpose? There is no reason why we should not set it down that God is truly and properly just.

Concerning the next point – how God exercises justice in this world – He will dispense the same goodness to our inferiors, equals and superiors. Since both equality and superiority are not possible in our relations with God, we can only expect at His hands the same justice that is given to those we regard as our inferiors. In this sense, God assumes the person of a judge, a lord, and a father.

'He shall judge the nations,' says the Prophet in the seventh Psalm. Because this seems to imply some future judgement with a truce for the present time, the wicked person is emboldened, takes heart and courage, refuses to be reformed, casts the words of God behind him, and runs on with his lost companions. The refrain of God in the Psalm restrains him not one whit from any evil deed, word or syllable that his heart delights to utter. He cares little for Christ's and the Apostle's divinely inspired and fearful admonition that God 'shall judge the nations'. [13]

— *God as Judge* —

For this reason, the prophet added these words: 'God not only will judge the nations' but He 'is the judge of the just and of the daily despisers of God'. [14] This means that what openly convicted criminals may look for is a judge who is no respecter of a person's rank, stands in awe of no one's image, profoundly hates sin, and knows every action and circumstance of a sinner's actions no matter how secretly executed. Let unrepentant wrongdoers make a clear reckoning of what they may expect from such a judge. For as surely as God is just, His justice will visit itself upon them sooner or later. If they experience that judgement before they fear it, woe unto them!

This God is their judge. But He is your Lord. So if you sincerely endeavour to serve and please Him, then you have a rightful claim to the benefits of His protection, preservation and all other good things His righteous dominion offers to those who serve Him. In the 33rd chapter of Isaiah, the Church concludes boldly and plainly on this point: 'He is our King, therefore He will save us.' [15]

It is not so much that you have permission to plead your case, as Hezekiah did when he said, 'Lord, remember how I have walked before you in truth with a perfect heart and have done that which is good in your sight.' Rather, with David, we should say, 'Preserve my soul, O Lord, for you are of great kindness unto all who serve you; save me for I am your servant. O Lord, enter not into judgement with your servant. Save your judgement for your enemies and those who hate you, but as for me, I am the son of your handmaid, your servant.' [16]

If the name 'Lord' does not seem sufficiently full of grace for you, then surely the Holy Spirit has given you courage to call upon God with a cheerful voice like children calling their father. Enlarge your hearts and there is no good thing you can desire that your father's indulgence does not invite you to expect from Him. If you thirst after consolation, behold, it is said, 'As one who is comforted by his mother, so will I comfort you.' If you wish endless hearty affection, it is said, 'I have loved you with everlasting love.' If you wish a prosperous and flourishing estate, it is said, 'I will be unto them as dew, they shall grow as the lily and fasten their roots like the trees of Lebanon; their branches shall spread and their beauty will be like the olive tree; they shall spring forth like corn and flourish like a pleasant vine.' [17]

It is not with God as it is with men whose titles show what they should be rather than what they are. God will not be called what

He is not. His name reveals His nature. If His affection were not fatherly the name Father would offend him. Fathers lay up treasures for their children. Fathers spend their days in work and their nights in planning how to enlarge the estates of their children. And have the sons of God a Father who is careless about whether they sink or swim? If fathers are provoked to anger, they do not convey an unappeasable wrath. Do not the tears of children as they confess their faults and crave pardon oftentimes wring tears from a father's eyes? We do not find God in Scripture so often rejoicing over the righteous as shedding forth tears of kindness in the bosoms of penitent sinners. In this way God is righteous and in this way He shows His righteousness.

Next, concerning this matter of divine justice, we consider how it is that, for lack of understanding of how God's justice works, there is much injury done both to us and to God. Because of this poor understanding, some people, beholding the impunity of sinners and the prosperity that often seems to result from sinfulness, think that all of this is repugnant to divine justice. Some people, noting a difference between those who die immediately after repenting of some great and grievous sin and others always leading honest, holy, virtuous and upright lives, wonder at the unfairness of both groups entering into the same bliss. They see an injustice here, a kind of punishment of those who live upright lives. Seeing that God is a just judge, they suppose they will be rewarded for all their good works as though they were not in themselves worthy of justification.

These people err by thinking that those things are against God's justice which are not. Others err by thinking that what is not against God's justice is. By not considering how contrary it is to God's justice to condemn a person, without there being a cause for such condemnation within the person condemned, they have misconstrued certain sentences in Scripture. They have done so at no small hazard to God's honour and their own comfort. They have wrongly concluded that people were predestined to endless torment simply because it was the will of God to have them endlessly tormented.

— When Good Things Happen to Bad People – and Vice Versa —

The wrong that people do to God for lack of a right understanding of the workings of His justice is nowhere clearer than in the complainings about the hard and heavy calamities of the righteous and the arrogant prosperity of the godless. Books both sacred and profane are filled with this kind of complaint. The reasons that induce men to find incongruity and even a kind of repugnance in God's justice are these. First, that sort of justice which we call distributive justice and define as yielding to each person what is due in accordance with differences in the quality of each person's life, is violated when persons who are not of equal virtue receive the same reward. For this reason Abraham said to God, 'Far be it from thee to slay the righteous with the wicked so that as the wicked are, so the righteous should also be. Far be it from thee.' [18]

If it is a condition most unequal and inconsonant with justice that those who excel in virtue should not be exalted in every aspect of happiness over those of a contrary sort, if it argues an uneven hand to bestow the same upon one sort as upon the other, what may we think of this? When those virtuous people whom all admire are among the worst off with respect to the outward things of life and at the same time are much complained of, while others live amidst the great abundance of whatever their hearts desire; and when the virtuous perish at the hands of their enemies, as they often do; and when they are found to live in such a way that even their deadliest adversaries would hardly wish upon them, is it not then reasonable to conclude that this is not what equity and justice require?

Secondly, our universally agreed upon sense of justice is that imprisonments, banishments, restraint of liberty, deprivation of rank, diminution of possessions, loss of life and limb, in fact anything penal and unpleasant, is to be meted out only to dangerous and deadly criminals. So that when the Supreme Guide and Governor of heaven and earth takes a completely contrary course of action, depressing and in all ways keeping down the good and virtuous and crowning the heads of malignants with honour and heaping happiness upon them, this can hardly seem to be just or righteous on His part.

It is understandable that objections have arisen among some who conclude that, if God did in truth order the course of human affairs, it should be *bonis bene malis male*, good for the good, bad for the bad. What are we to make of God's promises to the one sort and the other in His heavenly pronouncements: to the one group, 'If thou wilt walk in my ways and keep my ordinances and commandments I will lengthen and prolong your days,' and to the other, 'Thou O God shalt bring them down, thou shalt humble them unto the pit of corruption; bloody and deceitful men shall not live out half the time' allotted to them by nature? To the one is promised long life, prosperity and peace; to the other, not only unseasonable death but, before death, all sorts of misery.[19]

These being the words of God's own mouth, how do we see them performed when the righteous are 'hourly led like sheep to the slaughter' their goods taken from them by extortion, their persons subject to violence, driven to tears by all that befalls them, while impious 'despisers of God' rejoice in the pleasure of their beds, live long, grow old, increase in honour, authority and wealth, secure in their peaceful houses, the rod of God not upon them – not even near them?[20]

Can we square these things with God's word and our own condition? We might answer this question more easily and with greater equanimity if the harm done by such an inequitable situation were shown to produce some countervailing good. But so far as any man living can see, this is not so. The damage, loss and inconvenience which this confusion draws after it are apparent. For the benefits of just one person's virtue as it takes root and flourishes in the world are invaluable, not only with respect to the courage that other people draw from this visible example of one whose efforts to serve the Lord have produced good results, but also in the shared delight in being helpful to others and watching out for opportunities to do good. So it is that we bless such men as our common fathers and wish that they would possess heaven on earth.

On the other hand, there is no greater plague than dishonesty once it becomes longstanding and enables a person to annoy others. Dishonesty produces a scornful attitude towards the endeavours of virtuously disposed persons because it produces the thought, 'What profit have they who serve the Almighty?' Dishonesty makes it a recreation, a kind of sporting exercise, to see what can be devised to execute such vile, barbarous and cruel acts that future ages may wonder about and lament over this present age.

Since, therefore, nothing is more in harmony with the nature of God than the improvement of all things, what better way to fill the mouths of His saints with hymns of everlasting gratitude, to augment their joy, to demonstrate His glory, to silence His enemies for ever, to show all generations His concern for justice, than to make a clear and total separation between people according to their good and evil qualities?

These are the principal reasons why men perceive divine justice to be out of square when the righteous are afflicted and the wicked prosper. First, it seems to be against the rule of distributive justice that our condition should not vary according to the quality of our lives. Secondly, the general opinion and judgement of all people dislike it when such fairness is absent. Thirdly, God Himself has often and openly proclaimed that it should not be so. Finally, if this understanding of justice does not prevail, there will be great disturbances in the world. The virtuous will not be encouraged, but put out of heart and fail to perform the good works whereby thousands reap benefits. The wicked will be encouraged and emboldened to the dishonour of God and the discomfort of mankind.

It cannot be thought a needless labour to try to free this matter from confusion and provide a reasonable explanation for those who become entangled in the doubts caused by seeing a contradiction between God's justice and the needs of the world. First, we ask, how did we come to understand this rule of distributive justice, which requires that the condition of those of high virtue should be different from those of lower moral quality? Does justice require that the righteous have everything that is desirable and the unrighteous nothing that is good? If so, then that which no one was ever so senseless as to imagine would prevail, to wit, that God has dealt unjustly with the righteous. They alone are not beautiful, they alone are not strong, and they alone do not have heirs into the third and fourth generations.

According to this logic, see how unjustly God has dealt with our blessed Saviour, Christ, His only begotten Son, who, being so much more righteous than the angels, yet saw creatures far beneath Him rise above Him in outward honour and happiness, so far above Him that 'birds having nests and foxes holes to hide themselves, the Son of God and man had scarcely a place to lay his head'.[21]

— *Justice and Faith* —

Do we not know that God is by nature good and gracious to all the works of His hands? This means that the wicked deeds of men are their own acts, but as men they are still the work of God. Are we not doing them injury, rather than God injuring us, when we envy the good things they are capable of having? The favours which God gives to men not because they are men but because they are good, are so specially theirs that they can never be given to others. If you judge their condition, is it not as clear as light that the rule of distributive justice has not been violated in any way? It is most evident that God does not deal with the righteous the same as with the wicked, but always better.

For example, it would have been the height of childishness for Moses to 'choose a fellowship in the bitter afflictions of the people of God, refusing the offered pleasures of sin' if the just man's estate were not infinitely happier than that of the wicked man in his fanciest clothes.[22] Similarly, regard him who sits this very day in Rome [the Pope] with kings falling down before him, in his glittering estate. Does his triple diadem adorn him as honourably as the robes and garments dyed with the blood of martyrdom befitted his earliest predecessors who were disgraced, forsaken, banished, murdered, rent asunder, devoured by wild beasts, put to sharp and cruel deaths, subjected to every kind of torture for the name of Christ?

The poorest of them would not have exchanged their situations, even when in the midst of the greatest woe, for all the worldly joys and honours which the flourishing ranks of their successors acquired. When we think otherwise, the reason for our misconception is that, since all suffering is grievous and all pleasure is acceptable to the flesh, and since the unjust and the just suffer the same pain from hunger, pestilence, the sword, etc., we suppose that their suffering is all the same. In truth, their sufferings are different, both outwardly and essentially. The intention of God toward these two groups is never the same even though He seems to lay the same rewards and punishments on both. Although both are fired in the same furnace, one is as stubble, the other as gold. Being struck with the same rod, one receives torment as from a judge, the other chastisement as from a father. Being forsaken, they are not equally so, for one is forsaken because of a temporary abuse of his free will, the other because of a failure to recognize his state of damnation.

Therefore, the righteous may have their fantasies. They may be carried away with grief and be distempered with passionate feelings about how badly off they are. But surely there never was that hour in which, if mortal eyes could discern what true happiness is, even the unhappy would not wish with Balaam that they were as well off as the just and righteous.

And so the rule of distributive justice is not violated by God. As for the judgement of all the world to the contrary, of what account is that to us when we have the opinion of Him who created the world? Yet, we err if we take the casual and ill-advised words of those who utter rashly what indignation has put into their mouths rather than what sound reasoning has put into their minds to be the considered judgement of the world. For the wisest and most insightful of people, far from judging God negatively when the Saints were dealt with roughly and given the same treatment as those who were evil, plainly and authoritatively declared that the evils that befell the Saints were actually confirmations that assured them of everlasting bliss, rather than a sign that God makes no distinction between them and the children of the devil.

There is nothing enigmatic or obscure in the words of our Saviour, 'When men revile you, slander you, hate you, when they cast you out of their synagogues, when they speak and practise all manner of evil against you'[23] say not in your hearts that this is the fate that should have fallen on the wicked who don't know God. Their suffering does not mean that you will be unhappy. When you suffer these pains you are happy precisely because you suffer them. You may wonder why when you serve a God who is able to protect you, you are nevertheless made feeble and 'die daily'.[24] You are ignorant of how God brings it to pass that there is strength even in imbecility and gain in the very loss of your lives. Nor does anything done or suffered in this present world prejudice a whit the grand authority or impair the sacred credit, either of the promises of God concerning the good things of this life for those who serve Him, or of the threats of denunciation against the children of rebellion and disobedience.

That which befalls us in no way makes vain or frustrates what God has said. However, that which He has spoken and intended conditionally must be understood conditionally. The life of the just shall be long and fortunate, and they shall see many happy days and their prosperity will be a result of their piety, unless it is better for them to be otherwise. That suffering may be better for them requires no other proof than the testimony of men concerning the benefits of affliction. Minds that would be made immoral by prosperity are controlled by hard experiences. Affliction is the mother of hearty devotion.

'When God humbled their hearts with heaviness,' said the Prophet, speaking of Israel, 'then they cried unto the Lord; when they loathed and abhorred their food, then they poured out their very souls in supplication to God.'[25] Affliction is a medicine if we sin and a preservative against sinning. Again, if sentence of death and worldly calamity is given against those who hate to be reformed, we may be sure of their punishment, with the proviso that God is patient with sinners unless the remission of punishment would be less beneficial than its imposition. Who are we to allege that such examples of God's mercy and love towards mankind actually impede His righteousness? Yet we insist that we discern no apparent good resulting here, only many troubles.

'Truth', they say, 'is the daughter of time.' And who doubts that, in time, God may make clear that which we do not now understand? Must we deny that which we do not presently understand? Into the heart of Joseph, when his brothers sold him as merchandise, into the heart of Daniel, at the hour when he left his native soil, could the truth have penetrated that good would grow from such unpleasant beginnings? 'The end of all things', said the Apostle, 'is at hand.'[26] Until then, if the good that will result from what now seems confused in appearance lies buried 'in the bosom of God' alone, should we be less well informed about all this than that heathen Platonist who was uninstructed in the mysteries of our faith? 'In what I can understand concerning the works of God,' said Plato, 'therein will I praise him; and I will admire him even in those things which I know no reason for.' Do we not often affirm and do those things for which our wise men can see no reason?[27]

Neither should people dare to argue and dispute against God's actions simply because His intentions are hidden from them. As for the wicked, who hereby take this apparent delay in their punishment as occasion to harden themselves, it is to their greater woe in the end. Divine retribution shall come upon them so much the heavier, if slower. If the virtuous fail in courage because of their apparent misfortune in the short term, it is because of error and misunderstanding. 'There was a time', said the prophet David in the 73rd Psalm, 'when beholding fools in prosperity I fretted in my heart saying, Lo these are wicked yet they always prosper and increase in riches. Surely, in vain have I cleansed my heart and washed my hands in innocence. And to what purpose? Such was my ignorance; such my folly.'[28]

— *Justice in This Life and the Next* —

There is another sort who injure God in heaven because of their lack of understanding of how His righteous judgements operate upon those who repent their sins and await his mercy. They torment their minds with a fearful expectation of future anguish, tribulation and woe with the belief that however merciful God may be in remitting, pardoning and forgiving all their transgressions, He will be so unappeasable in the rigor of His corrective justice that, until they have endured in this world or the next punishments proportional to their pleasure in doing evil, their souls will never have rest.

Because much hangs on their false opinion, I will first endeavour to lay before you how the supporters and defenders of this view base it on a supposedly necessary condition of God's justice, and secondly to show you how weak and unfounded this argument is and how divine justice in no way requires such a condition but rather is utterly denied and contradicted by it.[29]

Those who cast but a slight view over this argument may think it strong and forceful. Such is the art and cunning with which it is constructed. The parts of the proposition are by their greatest proponents cemented and set together in this way: first, they say, quite rightly, that it is most true, and the root comfort of all Christians, that the death of our Lord and Saviour duly and sufficiently paid for the sins of the whole world by paying the price of redemption on the cross. Since such a solemn beginning cannot fail to have the full and ready agreement of all Christians, without further pause or deliberation they proceed smoothly with their argument by adding another point which cannot be reasonably denied, to whit, that no one ever partook of Christ's benefit except within the unity of the mystical body which is the Church.

To those within the fellowship of the Church, they argue, the streams of the holy blood of Christ and the beams of His grace are conveyed in various ways. Upon all persons at their first incorporation into the household of the faithful in Baptism the benefits of Christ's death are so fully conveyed that even if their lives were laden with the most enormous offences they are capable of in this life, yet they are not only pardoned but also perfectly acquitted for ever of all punishment and pain which their offences might deserve. Further, they argue that even if those who have been received into God's favour and the fellowship of his Church should sin after they have been baptized, in such a way as to pollute the temple of God, their condition is not irretrievable if they repent. They may be recovered through repentance because God has fully and mercifully promised His children who have erred and gone astray that if they return to Him and are penitent, He will grant them full remission of all their sins.

How can we find any deceit in those who begin with such weighty truths? Now that they have full possession of their listeners' minds, they slip into an idea which is utterly repugnant to the foregoing propositions but which they judge to be fully consonant and agreeable to them. Sin, once committed, they say, draws after it a double evil. First, it pollutes, defiles and stains the purity and dignity of our nature. Secondly, it makes the sinning soul immune to the punishment it deserves. To this we answer that God indeed does remit the many sins of His children when they heartily repent. Yes, they reply, He acquits them from the great pain of death and endless condemnation which they justly deserve. But, they say, it is an error to say that He always exempts those received into His grace from all corrective punishment.

In more ways than one, they argue, we see proof that God's justice exacts punishment for the offenders even after their offences have been forgiven. In the first place, have not just and holy men taken sharp revenge upon themselves for their sins? Has not the Church, in order to satisfy God's anger, from the very first spring of the Christian religion, always required certain penal works of transgressors? When people neither chastise themselves nor are chastised by the rod of the Church, God Himself punishes them whose sin He had pardoned. Was it not thus for our earliest progenitors whose grievous transgression was pardoned? Yet they smarted for that great sin, and so do we. For this cause the blessed Apostle spoke plainly to the people of Corinth, 'Do you not see how many there are among you who are weak and feeble, how many have fallen asleep,' some stricken with sickness, some with death? We might help ourselves if we were not so careless. 'If we judged ourselves, we would not be judged by God.' [30]

It cannot, therefore, be doubted, these papists wrongly argue, that there is pain due for sin even after the sin itself is forgiven. If any debt or recompense remains to be discharged by the offender after reconciliation with God, it increases in proportion with the number of faults committed. We cannot say that such debts are fully discharged in this life. How many thousands of sinners live securely at ease, altogether mindless of what they owe for their sins? How many, by reason of their late conversion to Christ, die before they can fully discharge their debt? If there were not sufficient pains for them to endure in the next life, those who sinned grievously at the end of life would be better off than those who committed small sins long before they died. This would be in keeping with God's justice unless we think that God would be forced to forgive such sin simply because He lacks the means to punish it in another world.

This false doctrine continues with the plea that the punishments that God has reserved for his children after this life are of two kinds: one is the absence of perfect happiness and bliss; the other a sensation of fearful and awful torments. In the former of these two states Adam and all the fathers until Christ's coming were detained in order to satisfy the punishment for sins that were forgiven in this life. Not only the holy patriarchs but also, with some exceptions, the souls of *all* the just lacked the abundant fruits of God's majesty in the next world. These departed souls, except for some who by special dispensation had already received their heavenly bliss and now rest in unbelievable happiness, lack any increase in joy and bliss so long as their bodies lie in the dust.

The other punishment in the next world, which has in it not only loss of joy but also a sense of grief, vexation and woe, is what they call the pain of purgatory. According to them, this is no different from the infernal torments endured by the souls of castaways and damned spirits except that there is an appointed term for the one group and no limit for the other. But for as long as they last, the torment is equal for both.

Nor should we think ourselves clearly and cleanly discharged of all such punishments just because we commit no heinous offences.

We are told that the common infirmities and daily trespasses which defile the works of the virtuous, such as immoderate laughter, excessive jesting, minor excesses in eating, drinking, clothing and the like, mind-wandering cogitations during holy services, are easily pardonable as venal oversights. But, it is said, if they are not forgiven here on earth, they must necessarily receive the punishment which justice requires in the afterlife. This, supposedly, is taught in Scripture, determined by the general Councils of the Church, believed by the ancient Fathers and even by the heathens acknowledged. Any doctrine which denies or doubts this truth, we are told, gives licence to evil-livers and is the very mother of pride.

We may reduce the entire sum of their false argument to two points. First, God's justice requires that, after the penitent sinner is forgiven, a suitable punishment for the sin must nevertheless be inflicted either by God or man. Secondly, if such punishment is not inflicted in this world, it will be in the world to come so that God's justice may be perfectly satisfied. For each of these two conclusions we have touched carefully upon the very flower of what the most wise and learned among the papists have alleged as proofs for us to stand upon. So that if what we have said on this subject is satisfying to reasonable persons, I hope we will not be thought unreasonable for withholding our assent to this whole thesis that which others urge upon the world with more eagerness than weight of argument.[31]

Notes

1. Psalms 34.12–22.
2. Habakkuk 2.4.
3. Hosea 2.21–22.
4. 'You shall not kill an uncondemned man.' 'If a patron wrongs his client he should be accursed.' From the sixteenth-century French *Corpus juris civilis* which was based on ancient Roman law.
5. Deuteronomy 13.1–5; 5.20; 19.16–21; Exodus 20.16.
6. From Job 19.17.
7. John 8.12–14; 1 Corinthians 4.1–5.
8. For the background of this story see W. Speed Hill, gen. ed., *The Folger Library Edition of the Works of Richard Hooker* Vols I–V (The Belknap Press of Harvard University, Cambridge, MA and London, 1977–1990), V, 820–1.

9. Here begins yet a third separate sermon usually included within 'A Learned Sermon on the Nature of Pride'. I have included it here because of its subject matter.
10. Exodus 33.18–19.
11. Psalms 115.3; Matthew 11.25–26; Ephesians 1.11.
12. Jeremiah 5.19.
13. Psalms 7.8.
14. Isaiah 2.4.
15. Isaiah 33.22.
16. Isaiah 38.3; Psalms 86.2, 5, 13, 16–17.
17. Isaiah 66.13; Jeremiah 31.3; Hosea 14.5–7.
18. Genesis 18.25.
19. 1 Kings 3.14; Psalms 55.23.
20. Romans 8.36; Acts 13.41.
21. Matthew 8.20; Luke 9.58.
22. Hebrews 11.24–25.
23. Matthew 5.11; Romans 1.30; Luke 6.22; John 16.2.
24. Romans 8.36.
25. Psalms 9.12; 106.44; 107.19; 142.2.
26. Daniel 1.6; 1 Peter 4.7; John 1.18.
27. The origin of the citation from Plato is unclear. See *Folger Edition*, V, 829.
28. Psalms 73.
29. Hooker here presents the best argument he can muster for a theory of God's justice with which he does not agree, namely that God punishes those he has already forgiven.
30. 1 Corinthians 11.30–32; John 12.47–48.
31. Hooker does not give us his own view of God's justice after death. By his denial of the preceding argument, he implies a non-vindictive God who does not punish in the next world those he has already forgiven in this life. This is consistent with his other statements about God's relation to the sinner.

— 8 —
Salvation

✵

I have combined three of Hooker's sermons here. They address a single theme – God's promise of salvation and our response to that promise. The first portion of what follows is traditionally known as 'A Sermon on Proverbs 3.9–10'. This, along with Hooker's 'A Sermon on Matthew 27.46' and 'A Sermon on Hebrews 2.14–15', are probably incomplete as we have them. Until the recent scholarship by Laetitia Yeandle and P. G. Stanwood in The Folger Library Edition of the Works of Richard Hooker, *all three were thought to be the work of the seventeenth-century Archbishop James Ussher of Armagh (1581–1656), who was a collector of Hooker's manuscripts. They had, in fact, been published as such in an edition of Ussher's works. Although we now know that the sermons are Hooker's, we are indebted to the scholarly Archbishop for having transcribed them from the originals and preserved them for posterity.*[1]

Any attempt to date these sermons is speculative. However, the pastoral tone and the focus on matters of concern to ordinary people make it a convenient guess that all three were delivered at Bishopsbourne during Hooker's years there, between 1595 and 1600.

— *God's Covenant With His People – One at a Time*[2] —

> ***Honour the Lord with your substance, and the first fruits of your increase [. . .] So shall your barns be filled with plenty; and your presses shall burst out with new wine.***[3]

To the precept of honouring the Lord with our riches and our principal revenues, Solomon added the promise that by so doing we will increase the very treasure which we seem to diminish in His service.

To understand this we must first consider what connection there is between the promise and the duty attached to it; second, the special assurance of treasure given to each particular person; third, the types of riches Solomon refers to; fourth, the extent of the rewards; fifth, how this will all work out in practice.

Is the lesson here that our bellies must first be filled before we will serve God? No. But it is true that the cares and needs we have in this world are the greatest obstacle keeping our minds from aspiring to heavenly things. Therefore, this promise is made to assure us that the best way to satisfy our needs is to honour God. He will not allow those who honour Him to be worse off because of their service to Him than they otherwise would have been.

The only thing that cools our ardour and affection for the required duty is something we prefer to keep secret.[4] Indeed, we are taught to do so. But when we have diminished our substance by service to God, where shall we go to supply the necessities of this life? The answer given here is that God's purpose in exacting this service from us is not to impoverish but to enrich His servants. In fact, He will multiply and increase their store of all things.

This does not mean that our service earns us such generosity at God's hands. That He rewards His servants comes not from the worthiness of our deeds, but from His goodness. By the rich and unspeakable wisdom of His providence, the world and everything therein is given to us so that as we serve God so will all other things serve Him, each in their own degree and order. On the other hand, if we swerve aside from our service to God, the Lord will be unkind to us. Whereas our godliness had resulted in the promises of life now and the life to come, so our contempt of God changes both the one and the other to the contrary fruits of accursedness and malediction.

So we may set it down as a solid axiom that when we denigrate and transgress our duty to God, which by our very nature we are supposed to observe, we lose the benefits which the things of this world, each working according to its own nature, might otherwise have yielded to us. God then restrains the fruits of the earth in such a way that they may or may not easily supply the desires and needs of men.

That God does in any way enlarge or restrict the powers of the natural world needs no proof – only some reflection. All the Scriptures give witness to this fact. For example, when famine threatened God's children, Scripture shows that by repentance and prayer these evils are removed. Even the heathens, by making supplications to God in the midst of their various needs, have acknowledged His power to control the forces of nature.

I will delay no longer opening up to you the connection between God's promise and our duty to respond. Consider the special assurance of this connection given to each of us in the words of the author of Proverbs, 'Honour the Lord with your substance and you shall be replenished; your presses shall burst with new wine.' Or recall God's promise to His people in the second chapter of Hosea, 'I will hear the heavens, and the heavens shall hear the earth, and the earth shall hear the corn, wine and oil, and they shall hear Israel.'[5]

If the implication here was only that God has made a general provision for His chosen people, that the country where they dwell will yield what is sufficient for them, but that this promise does not apply to each particular person's estate and welfare, that would be poor comfort, a slender encouragement. If such were the case, God would have less regard for His family than an earthly father whose care extends to each particular person, no matter how mean his condition. As Solomon says, 'A just man is not careless, no not even of the least who labour for him.'[6]

For this reason, God's spirit singles out each of us separately, speaking to us, as it were, one by one, so that no one may doubt that he will reap with his own hands the fruits of his religious service. [. . .][7]

— *The Saviour*[8] —

That through death He might break the power of him who had death at his command – that is the devil – and might

liberate those who, through fear of death, had all their lifetimes been in servitude. Hebrews 2.14–15

God gave His people, the Jews, a law which is set down in the 25th chapter of Leviticus, that at the end of every seven-times-seven years, which totals 49, the next or fiftieth year should be a year of jubilee. This year is to have two special requirements: first, the free restitution of all lands that were the ancient inheritance of men who have subsequently lost them; secondly, the full release from all obligation of those who have been in debt bondage to others. People deprived of freedom, bereft of hereditary goods and possessions, held in bondage, or enclosed in dangerous prisons, were to be set free at this time. In the jubilee year they were all restored to a state of such perfect liberty that no one might challenge or charge them for past offences. This jubilee was a prefiguring of a greater jubilee yet to come.[9]

The angel Gabriel, in the ninth chapter of Daniel's prophecy, calculated that from the time of the edict of Cyrus concerning the Jews' return to their homeland (which was probably in a jubilee year) until the time of our Saviour Christ was 500 years, containing ten jubilees.[10] This was the term of years that God had set to 'finish transgressions, to bring an end to sin, to extinguish iniquity, to endure everlasting righteousness, to seal up vision and prophecy, to anoint the most holy'. Then the prophet added that the 'Messiah should be slain, and not for himself.' If not for Himself, then for whom?[11]

The prophet Isaiah (53rd chapter) shows for whom He is to be slain: 'Surely for *our* infirmity he has borne and carried *our* sorrows; he was wounded for *our* transgressions, broken for *our* iniquities; for the transgression of *my* pride he was plagued.'[12] His death was the price for our salvation; the days of His sorrow have brought to us the joy of a jubilee that has no end: the benefits of perfect deliverance from slavery and restitution of that inheritance that Satan required of our parents.

Thus we are made free, saved and redeemed from our bonds. We are made sons, co-inheritors with our Redeemer. To Him let the tongues of men and angels sound for ever that blessed hymn, written for this very purpose, 'Praise and honour and glory and might to him who sits on the throne and to the Lamb for ever and ever.'[13]

Thus you see why both Christ and the Apostles, in order to describe the fruits of His death and passion, speak at length about inheritance and deliverance from slavery. Concerning all the miraculous works that have occurred since the world began, there is not one that can be compared with what our Lord and Saviour did through His death. He frustrated the very sovereignty of death, making its power of no effect. [. . .]

After noting the means by which Christ defeated Satan, the second thing we should observe is the benefit of deliverance resulting therefrom; third, the number of people affected; fourth, the enslaved condition of those who were set free by Christ; fifth, their fear of death; and last, the continuation of that fear, lasting throughout their entire lives.

The very centre of Christian belief, the life and soul of Christ's Gospel, rests in this: that by ignominy, honour and glory is obtained; power is vanquished by imbecility; and, by death, salvation is purchased.

No Jew ever doubted that a Messiah would come and that he would save and redeem the world. It has always been, and is to this day, an article of their creed that 'God in the end of the days shall send our Messiah . . .' Upon this article of the Jewish faith, Moses proclaimed, 'Whosoever doubts this point accuses the whole law of falsehood.' All Jewish prophecy expressly and clearly requires that we put our trust and confidence in that anointed One.[14]

From whence is their blindness who are so hardened against the Gospel of Jesus Christ? There is no other cause but this. The Jews cannot stand to hear that their saviour would bring life and salvation through his death and passion. Their belief has always been that their saviour should be a king over all the earth and that by force of arms he would bring the world under his control. That is what Herod believed and that is why he was vexed, molested, and troubled by the birth of our Lord. Thus did all nations and peoples believe who had heard the Jewish prophecies.

Jesus' own disciples had the same idea when they asked Him, 'Lord, when will you restore again the kingdom of Israel?' and when they made their vain and aspiring requests to sit on His right or left hand, and when they contended to see who should be the greatest among His disciples. These questions all sprang from the same root. It was not until Christ was dead, raised again, and ascended to His Father that the right understanding of the ancient prophecies came to light. Until then, even the disciples never imagined that death was the means whereby such great things would be accomplished. It was in this sense that the Apostle referred to the Gospel as 'a mystery, hidden since the beginning of the world, concealed from former ages and never opened before, but now made manifest to the Saints of God'.[15]

Might not the Son of God, who had the power to create and sustain the world, deliver His people by His great strength? Could Satan have held captive those whom the Son of Man had made free? The answer to this question may be clearer if we refer it to the next point in our discussion by examining the benefit resulting from Christ's action, namely, our deliverance, our salvation. In the first place, since God is filled with justifiable indignation and wrath towards us, what other way is there to reconcile us but through the intercession of Him who has received God's highest favour? In our Saviour's death is combined the highest degree of honour and the lowest degree of humiliation.

If we enter into the search for what God intends to reveal to us, we can find a thousand testimonies to show that the whole scope of Christ in the work of our deliverance was to display the treasures of His own infinite love, goodness, grace and mercy. 'My sheep I know; I give them eternal life. They shall never perish neither shall any pluck them out of my hands.'[16] That is to say, God delivered them.

This act of God was sufficient to express the benefit of our deliverance, but not sufficient to express His love, and so He added, 'Behold, I lay down my life for them.' [. . .] Indeed, the principal thing which our Grand Deliverer would have us forever remember is 'that by death He has wrought our deliverance'. For this reason the Sacrament of the Holy Eucharist was instituted so that the breaking of flesh and the shedding of blood, that is to say, the very face of death itself, would appear within it.[17] [. . .]

— *The Saved* —

We should not overlook the third point in this discussion concerning the magnitude of this benefit called salvation, which is made available by our God for many people. If anyone is deprived of deliverance, the fault is his own. Let no one, therefore, probe the clouds to look for secret impediments to his salvation. Let them not, like the infidels and heathens, stormily impute their wretched condition to destiny. *Fatis agimur, credite fatis.*[18] Let not such ideas inhabit anyone's thoughts. Abandon them with all denunciation and hatred as impious, diabolical thoughts. Satan himself should not plead that there was ever any child of perdition who was excluded from salvation through the death of Jesus, except by the malice of his own contrary will. [. . .] The fatal bar that closes the door to God's saving mercy is only our wilful contempt of the grace and salvation offered to us.

Upon this sure foundation let us, therefore, build. Christ died to deliver us *all*. Let not the subtlety of Satan beguile you with fraudulent expectations and drive you into such labyrinths or mazes, as your wit cannot enter without losing itself. You have the plainly expressed words of our Lord and Saviour inviting all unto Him who labour.[19] You have the blessed Apostle's express assertion that Christ by His death defeated Satan, to the end that He might deliver *all* who are held in bondage. Urge this upon yourself: God cannot deny Himself. He preaches deliverance, by His death, for *all*.[20]

If, therefore, any are not delivered it is because they have said to their own hearts: 'Our present pleasures will remain our god; we care not for this offered favour; we will not have Him to be our deliverer.' If such as these perish, what eye is there to pity them?

And, if any ever do perish, it will be such as these, be they Jew, Greek or heathen.

Our state of being before deliverance, as the Apostle notes on our fourth point, is a state of bondage, servitude and slavery. We know that the word servant applies to all who must follow the command of another and that there is only one Lord who has the power to command all of us. But here the Apostle is referring to servants who are miserable, unfortunate and wretched in their servitude, and that does not refer to those who serve God. The Lord who is served in such a case must, therefore, be fierce, savage and tyrannical. [. . .] The misery of this sort of servitude lies in the vileness of the work the slaves must do because they cannot withstand the unreasonable commands of their master. [. . .] Speaking of this lord who is served by the unsaved, the Apostle Paul says, 'They that are such serve not the Lord Jesus Christ but their bellies.' In another place he says, 'Such were we ourselves in times past, serving lusts and every kind of pleasure.'[21]

But how vile is this labour which these evil lords demand of their servants? The trade and course of their lives St Peter compares (as you know) to the wallowing of swine in mire that is loaded with dog vomit. Their very food is such that the heart of man abhors and loathes thinking about.[22]

Notwithstanding the truth of all this, those who live in this sort of ghastly servitude and are bound irrevocably with such chains are in one particular unlike other slaves. They do not feel their misery. Their servitude seems sweet to them because they do not see it as such.

It is the purpose of all tyrants to assure that those who are most oppressed by them will not seem to be oppressed. Therefore, in tyrannical kingdoms we see that the doors of men's lips and their glances are jealously observed lest by pouring forth their mutual complaints they become aware of their misery and begin to plot how to shake off the yoke that lies heavily upon them. That which tyrants can't accomplish, Satan brings to pass in his subtle way. Knowing that as soon as those who serve him begin to become aware of their servitude they will refuse to remain slaves, Satan's intention is to keep them hoodwinked and to nourish those fantasies that lead them to think that they are the freest people in the world.

Thus it is that such people willingly discharge their service to Satan, even sinning with a kind of greediness. Compare them with the best or the simplest attendants in the courts of our God. Note that their effort to do good is cold and sluggish when compared to the subtle evil done by the followers of Satan. Our Saviour Christ, at the time of His greatest agony, had no one near Him to hold up His head, no one to watch Him in prayer; no, not even Peter. Only Judas, as servant of Satan, spent a sleepless night.

Spiritual servitude would be severe enough if it had no other evil attached to it but the indignity of living such a base and ignominious life. But this is not all. The Apostle adds that they also live in fear.[23] Fear pertains to those ends yet to come. It is a trembling perturbation of the mind, arising from the preconception of some immediate harm which threatens grievous affliction of the sort that our nature cannot easily bear or sustain.

The difference between the slave and the freeman is this: the things most dreadful to those ransomed and freed by Christ are in the past; but for the unsaved, the worst is forever what is yet to come. [. . .] Miseries escaped are not miseries. They serve only to comfort us and make us thankful to Him by whose mercy we escaped them. As for the servants of Satan, however, they may seem to flourish for a time and are accounted by others and even themselves to be fortunate, nevertheless, 'at their end, they mourn'.[24] [. . .]

Is not the most common disease among the wretched a false security, as if the evil that threatens them were but idle and empty words? The Apostle's meaning, therefore, cannot be that their whole life on earth is to be, as it were, a continual fever and their souls possessed with perpetual trembling. Rather, his words are directed to those who know something about what is waiting for them in the world to come, as slaves of sin and Satan. Because they know it, it is evident to them that this life is nothing but a daily approaching, nearer and nearer, of the consequences in that heavy hour, which they have every reason to fear, however little they may be troubled by those consequences today. (By 'fear' we are to understand the danger of falling into that which is rightly feared, whether we are actually fearful or not.)

— *Fear of Death* —

So long as we live in this miserable state of servitude, in which estate we do live until such time as that word of promise (which is God's salvation to all who truly and heartily embrace it and is also a message which brings tidings of grace, mercy, pardon, peace and reconciliation), and until such time as that truth which alone has the power to free our spirits, has freed us, it is impossible for us to draw a free breath. This is because we are at every moment at risk of death. And a fearful thing it is to lie bound tightly by the chains of this kind of slavery.

Death, considered in itself, is an enemy. [. . .] Because death has as yet the upper hand against all of us, it is natural to fear it. Those who speak of death solely from a natural perspective can only decide that it is entirely terrible. This natural horror of death is heightened in many ways. [. . .] There are even virtuous desires to do good in this world that can make a person unwilling to leave the world and consequently afraid of death. But those whose death is but a speedy entrance into a second and endless dying have the most reason to fear death, although many times these people are the ones who fear it least.

Even as there are many factors that aggravate, so there are many that abate, the fear of death. Sometimes this fear is extinguished by a bad and impious disposition, as with desperate godless persons who care as little about what they may suffer as about what they do. Or death may be acceptable to whomever despairs and has lost patience with life. These are violent smotherings of fear which can only be conquered by the strength of right reason which can cause the will to yield contentedly and stay alive, even when nature or duty seems to demand death.

The main reason why the heathens were so resolved to die were those offered by Seneca to the effect that with death comes an end to indefinite troubles and molestations, or by Aristotle who saw death as beneficial to the whole world. Birth stops death, he said, and death gives way to birth. Therefore, we should be content to give place to others by our death, even as by our birth we succeeded others who had died.[25]

The truest weapon we have to strike back against the natural terrors of death is the submission we owe to God's will, at Whose commandment our readiness to die shows that we are called from this stage of life as His sons, and not as servants. Those who lived as sons, being dead, are blessed. The pains that they suffered here are now ended, the evil that they did is buried with them, and their good works follow them. Their souls are safe in the hands of God. Not even their bodies are lost but are laid up for them.

— *God's Awful (but Tempered) Judgement*[26] —

My God, my God, why hast Thou forsaken me? Matthew 27.46

There are two forms of God's rejection of man. The first is complete and total rejection. The second is rejection that serves only as a trial or test of our faith.

Complete rejection involves the soul in its everlasting nature. It occurs when God, in His justifiable displeasure, denies the grace of His saving mercy to those whose behaviour has made them unacceptable vessels of His goodness. Those who were truly born of Him are never, in this sense, totally forsaken by God. On the contrary, they have His sweet and comfortable promises to rely upon. They have the promises of Scripture. Isaiah says: 'For a moment in anger I hid my face from you for a little season; but with everlasting mercy I have compassion for you, says the Lord, your Redeemer; the mountains shall move and the hills shall fall down, but my mercy shall not depart from you, neither shall the covenant of my peace fall away, says the Lord.'[27] Jeremiah says, 'I shall make an everlasting covenant with them that I will never turn away from doing them good; I will put my fear in their hearts and they shall not depart from me';[28] John says, 'He loved his own [. . .] to the end.' John also says, 'The seed of God remains in them.'[29]

On the other hand, no child of God is exempt from the second kind of rejection. Even God's own Son, that Son of whom He proclaimed with a thundering voice from heaven, 'This is my beloved Son in whom I am well pleased,' was rejected, but only for a time and not totally.[30]

God's rejection of Christ was only of His human nature. It affected only His body and the part of His soul wherein His passions and emotions resided. The intellectual part of Jesus' soul, the part where reason, judgement, wisdom, the comprehension of truth, and the light of God shone could not possibly be extinguished.

When Christ cries out, 'My God, my God,' the strong sinews of His words and the force and vigour of His speech show us that He has clasped God with a fast embrace, and that God already abides in His fortress – the very pinnacle and turret of Christ's soul.

We recall that God left the body of Job for Satan to work upon; but he did not allow Satan to take Job's life. In the case of our Lord and Saviour, Satan and his imps were permitted to beat upon Christ's body like an anvil and to assault His senses with whatever wit and malice they could invent. His eyes they wounded with the spectacle of scornful looks, His ears with the sound of heinous blasphemies, His taste with gall, the feeling throughout His body with such tortures as blows, thorns, whips, nails and spear could breed, until His soul was finally chased out of Him like a bird. So, insofar as the pain and destitution inflicted on His body was concerned, Jesus might well have uttered those words that we find in the doleful lament of Jeremiah (Lamentations 1.12), 'All ye that pass by and behold, see if ever there were sorrow like unto my sorrow, with which the hand of the Lord hath afflicted me.'[31]

That lower part of the soul that houses imagination and affection, fear and depression, was so afflicted as to turn sweat into drops of blood and to cause a thrice-repeated plea for escape from this pain. Who can imagine what He was feeling at the hour when He cried out, 'Thou hast forsaken me'? What man can imagine such agony? Our imagination is too limited to plumb the depths of this mystery.

Neither may we suppose that Satan, who had been so assiduous in assaulting His body, failed to beset His soul with legions of the most grisly terrors and fears. In the past, angels had been sent from heaven to comfort Jesus. But at this hour, neither God, nor angels, nor man came to ease His heavy heart with the comfort of their presence. Instead, a curtain was drawn between the passionate powers of His soul and whatever might bring Him relief and refreshment. 'O Thou afflicted and tossed with tempest!' Who can hear this mournful cry of Christ and not feel that their own soul has been scorched, without leaving a single drop of the moisture of joyful feeling?

But I foolishly labour here to explain what cannot really be explained. Our best response to this awful mystery is an amazed silence.

Notes

1. For the provenance of these three sermons, see W. Speed Hill, gen. ed., *The Folger Library Edition of the Works of Richard Hooker* Vols I–V (The Belknap Press of Harvard University, Cambridge, MA and London, 1977–1990), V, 395–8. See also P. G. Stanwood and Laetitia Yeandle, 'Three Manuscript Sermon Fragments by Richard Hooker', *Manuscripta*, 21 (1977), 33–7.
2. Known traditionally as 'A Sermon on Proverbs 3.9–10'.
3. Proverbs 3.9–10.
4. Hooker may be referring to greed.
5. Proverbs 3.9–10; Hosea 2.21–22.
6. Proverbs 12.10.
7. The remainder of the sermon is missing.
8. This portion of the sermon is usually called the 'Sermon on Hebrews 2.14–15'.
9. Leviticus 25.8–12.
10. This edict by the King of Persia in 538 BC was for the rebuilding of the Temple and the return of the Jews to Jerusalem.
11. Hooker no doubt refers here to Daniel's vision in chapters 10–12. See Daniel 9.21–23, 24, 26.
12. Isaiah 53.4–5.
13. Revelation 5.13.

14. The creed of Maimonides (1135–1204) was a basis for the Jewish belief in a messiah who would save the faithful. See Joseph Hertz, *The Authorized Daily Prayer Book* (Block Publ. Co., New York, 1996), 6–7. See *Folger Edition*, V, 841–2 for further commentary.
15. Acts 1.6; Matthew 20.20; Luke 22.24–27; Hebrews 2.9, 14–15; Romans 5.10; 6.3; Colossians 1.26; 2.3.
16. John 10.27–28.
17. John 10.17; Colossians 1.13; Romans 4.25.
18. 'By fate we are driven; yield to fate.' Seneca, *Oedipus* I.980.
19. Matthew 11.28.
20. Hooker's use of the word 'all' is provocative. It suggests that he flirted with the heretical idea of universal salvation.
21. Romans 16.18; Titus 3.3.
22. Ephesians 5.12; 2 Peter 2.22; Proverbs 26.11.
23. Hebrews 2.15.
24. Proverbs 5.11.
25. For commentary on Hooker's use of Seneca and Aristotle in this passage, see *Folger Edition*, V, 847–8.
26. This segment, on a somewhat tangential subject, is traditionally titled, 'A Sermon on Matthew 27.46'.
27. Isaiah 58.8, 10.
28. Jeremiah 32.40.
29. John 13.1; 10.18; 1 John 3.9.
30. Matthew 3.17; 17.5.
31. Lamentations 1.12.

— 9 —
The Pathway to God[1]

This is surely one of Hooker's most beautiful, coherent and compelling sermons. Rooted firmly in Holy Scripture, it offers a road-map to God and a culminating celebration of God's love. In the timeless words of St James, Hooker proclaims that our God is a 'generous giver'.

The date and place of the writing and presentation of this sermon are unknown. The piece was not always acknowledged as Hooker's despite Isaac Walton's attribution of it to him in his 1678 Life of Bishop Sanderson. *The first publication was when Walton appended it to that work. The sermon, he said, had been found in Bishop Lancelot Andrewes' study. That distinguished bishop had been one of those entrusted with Hooker's unpublished writings shortly after he died in November 1600. In the editions of Hooker's writings after Walton's publication of the sermon it did not appear again, until John Keble included it in his 1836 edition. It is included in the* Folger Library Edition *of his works.*[2]

> ***Ask and it shall be given to you. Seek and you shall find. Knock and it shall be opened to you. Whoever asks*** . . .
> Matthew 7.7

Even as all creatures that attain their highest perfection in the fullness of time are at their beginning raw, so man, who is closest to perfection when at the end of his race, is at the entrance to life so weak that he is forced to depend on the voluntary good will of those who have no reason to help him except the secret inclination to repay to the common stock of humanity the help they once needed and borrowed. In this, the condition of all flesh is the same.

Although there is in us when we are born no idea or apprehension of our own misery and for a long time thereafter no inclination to seek help at the hand of others, yet through God's most gracious providence, the God who feeds the feathered souls of young birds (whose needs are famously noted in Scripture) hears our prayers and supplications.

We, whom God values more highly than millions of brute creatures, find daily occasions regularly to acknowledge with the Prophet David, 'You, O Lord, from our birth have been merciful to us.' We have tasted your goodness hanging 'even at our mothers' breasts'. That God who during infancy preserves us without our knowledge teaches us as we mature how to use our own abilities to achieve our own good.[3]

> Ask and it shall be given you, seek and you shall find, knock and it shall be opened to you. For, whoever asks shall receive, whoever seeks shall find and the door shall be opened to everyone who knocks.[4]

In these words we are first commanded to *ask*, *seek* and *knock*. Secondly, we are promised grace as a response to each of these endeavours: asking we shall have, seeking we shall find, knocking, it shall be opened to us. Thirdly, this grace applies in particular cases because it is implied that no one who is sincerely asking, seeking and knocking will fail to achieve what he desires.

— *Asking (Praying)* —

About asking (praying) I do not need either to tell you at whose hands we must seek our aid or to remind you that our hearts are those golden censers from which the fumes of this fragrant incense of prayer must ascend. For you know who it is who said, 'Call upon me.' We also know that God wants our hearts, for He said, 'Son, let me never fail in my duty to have your heart.'[5]

Against the invocation of any other than God alone, there are many forcible arguments. If all else fails, this stark and singular challenge may suffice: God in Scripture gave us so many patterns to imitate when we pray and gave us ready-made supplications for every condition and need in our lives, and there is not one, no not one, prayer directed to angels, saints or anyone except God alone. Should we not feel safe in this matter and be led by the best examples in our tradition, conforming our prayers to what Noah, Abraham, Moses, David, Daniel, and all the rest prayed, indeed that form of prayer that Christ himself taught His Church and that blessed Apostles practised? [. . .]

Whoever comes to God with the gift of prayer must do so with a cheerful heart, with a free and frank affection. Devotion and earnestness add to prayer in the same way that timeliness adds to gifts; they put vigour and life into them.

Prayer proceeds from need, which, being heart-felt, makes the suppliant eager. This eager insistence was not only tolerated by our Saviour Christ, as the story of the woman of Canaan, in Matthew 15, shows, but also encouraged, as we see in the parable of the wicked judge in Luke 18. Our fervency shows us to be sincerely desirous of what we crave but that which will make us capable of it is a humble spirit. For 'God bestows His grace upon the lowly; but the proud He sends away empty.'[6]

Therefore, to the end that all generations might know how important it is to beware of all lofty and vain egotism when we are offering up our prayers to God, He has given in His Gospels this caveat in the form of a parable: the Pharisee and the tax collector, having presented themselves in the Temple of God to perform the common duty of prayer, differed from one another to such an extent that our Lord's verdict about them is a matter of public record. 'They departed for home,' said the Lord, the sinful tax collector in humility born of his good prayer, the Pharisee in sin, born of his prideful prayer.[7] [. . .]

Asking would be easy if that were all that God required. But because there are ways appointed by His providence for us to attain what He would give us and because those means are sometimes so complicated as to require deliberation, study and wit, he that summits a supplication may expect an inquisition. Prayer is difficult work.

The baits of sin lie everywhere, readily available to us, whereas that which is precious is hidden and not obtainable unless sought after. Straightness and roughness are the qualities of every good and perfect way. What good is it to others if we wish them well and do nothing to help them? Similarly it avails us little if we pray but do not seek. To trust in works without prayer signifies impiety and blasphemy. We make light of the providence of God (though this may be unintentional) and show a lack of mature judgement when we pray in a lazy manner without exerting any effort. He who said, 'if any man lacks wisdom, let him ask,' has in the same manner commanded us 'to seek wisdom, and to search for understanding as for a treasure'.[8] To those who merely craved a seat in the kingdom of Christ, His answer in the Gospel was, as you know, 'To sit at My right hand and My left hand in the seat of glory is not a gift in return for services rendered but a divine assignment from God.' Christ liked better the man who inquired, 'Lord, what shall I do that I might be saved?' He directed him to the right and ready way to labour: 'Keep the commandments.'[9]

— *Seeking* —

I spoke to you earlier of certain special qualities that mark those who *ask*. In those who *seek* there are also qualities that we may observe. With many of them it is as with those of whom the Apostle spoke in Second Timothy 3.7: they 'are always hearing and never able to come to the knowledge of truth'[10] because, as St Bernard said, '*Ex amore non quaerunt*, they seek because they are merely curious and not because they wish to be obedient.'[11] It was distress and perplexity of mind that made some people inquisitive. St Luke reported in Acts that when men seek counsel and advice with urgent prayer God blesses them with the spirit of understanding. They should not hide from less fortunate persons the knowledge that would show them what they must do to gain eternal life.[12]

That which our Saviour says about praying in public, causing trumpets to play when we give alms, and making service to God a means to win the praise of everyone must be applied here to those who never seek as they ought to unless they have a company of onlookers. 'On my bed,' said the faithful in the Canticles, 'there did I seek the One my soul loves.'[13]

Therefore, when you resolve to seek do not go out of your house into the street but avoid places of distraction. Separate yourself from yourself, if such is possible. When you seek let the love of obedience, the sense and feeling of necessity, and the eye of sincere meaning guide your footsteps and you will not slide.

— *Knocking* —

Now you see what it is to ask and seek. The next step is to *knock*. There is always in every good thing for which we ask and which we seek some large wall, some barred gate, some strong impediment or other intruding itself between us and our goal. To remove these impediments we need the help of stronger hands than our own. Just as asking relates to our desire for good things and seeking relates to the natural and ordinary means of attaining them, so knocking is necessary to overcome the hindrances or impediments which are closed up against us like doors, until such time as it pleases the goodness of almighty God to open them.

In the meantime our duty is to knock. Many are well contented to ask and not unwilling to take some pains in seeking. But, as soon as they see obstacles that flesh and blood judge to be invincible, their hearts are broken.

When the people of Israel were in Egypt, subject to the miseries of intolerable servitude, they craved with sighs and tears to be delivered from a condition they were fully persuaded they could not change, except for the better. To be set free to seek the land which God had promised to give their fathers did not seem tedious or irksome to them. They undertook this difficult journey with all speed, never troubled with doubt or dismayed by fear until at length they came to that solid door. They had no means, and so no hope, of breaking the bars on the door.

Mountains on this side, the roaring sea before their faces, and all the forces that Egypt could muster coming at them with all the fury and rage that could possibly possess the heart of a proud and cruel tyrant. In these straits, at this instant, they despaired: O that we had been so lucky as to have died. Before this we lived a life that was toilsome but free of the extremities we have fallen into now. Is this the 'milk and honey' that was so often spoken of? Is this the paradise on which so much deceptive eloquence has been spent? Have we, after 430 years, left Egypt to come to this? While the people of Israel were in the midst of these mutinous thoughts, Moses, with all urgency, beat upon the door and God, with his powerful hand, cast open the gates before them, despite their infidelity and despair. [14]

It was not strange then or later on that the Israelites were in such a dissatisfied state. Until they came to the very brink of the river Jordan, the least difficulty that lay in their path was always a reason for recidivism or relapse. Yes, even having the promised land in their possession, being situated in the heart of it, and with all of their worst hardships behind them, Joshua and the best of their governors, who had seen the wonders that God had done for His people, had no sooner ended their days when first one tribe and then another, delighted in their prosperity, fearful to trouble themselves by following God's commands, weary of passing through so many straight and narrow gates, gave in to ignominious terms of peace, joined hands with infidels, and forsook Him who had always been the rock of their salvation. As a result, no more doors opened to them despite their knocking with greater energy than ever before.

Concerning Issachar, the words of Jacob, the father of all patriarchs, were these: 'Issachar though muscular and strong enough to do any labour, lives like an ass. He thinks to himself that a permanent house is good and the land is pleasant. So he bent his back to the burden and submitted to forced labour and the paying of tribute, rather than casting himself into the hazards of war.' [15] We are, for the most part, of Issachar's disposition. We account our laziness cheap at any price. Although we can sometimes get ourselves into a frame of mind to ask, or even occasionally endure the labour of seeking, we are loath to follow a course of life that might hem us in with great uncertainties and dangerous risks.

— *God's Promises* —

Concerning our duties to ask, seek, and knock, I have said sufficient. Now, let us look at what God promises to those who do so.

'Ask and receive; seek and find; knock and it shall be opened to you.' Promises are made here of good things to come. While we wait for them we fear a painful process. But when they are performed and bear fruit, we experience joy. Abraham rejoiced, to some extent, in what he saw was coming even though he knew that many ages and generations must first pass. The exultation was to be far greater for those who beheld Jesus with their own eyes and embraced with their arms the Saviour who, in earlier times, had been only the hope of the world. We have found the Messiah, seen our salvation. 'Behold, here is the Lamb of God who takes away the sins of the world.' These are the words of men not merely comforted by the hope of what they seek but enthralled by the experience of bliss. [16]

Whenever our experience of God's abundant mercy toward us is the same as the prophet David's, we should offer the same acknowledgement that came from his mouth: 'I called on the name of the Lord and He rescued his servant. I was in misery and He saved me. You, Lord, have delivered my soul from death, my eyes from tears, and my feet from falling.' [17] I have asked and received, sought and found, knocked and it has been opened to me.

Can anything less be expected from us than to take into our hands *the cup of salvation*, to bless, magnify and extol His mercies heaped upon the heads of the sons of men (Psalm 116)? Are we like those who merely ask and so do not receive? We shall rejoice, then, but how? We shall find, but where? It shall be opened, but with what hands? To all these questions, I answer with the words of our Saviour Christ, 'What are these things to us?' [18]

Is it up to us to understand the way God brings His words and purposes about? God does nothing without the use of certain means and instruments but these methods may be those which seem to us most unlikely. This does not mean that, under cover of trusting in God, we should nourish a posture of idleness. Nor does it mean that we should offer God sacrifices of prey we have taken in nets of our own weaving, simply because these offerings are easy to come by and commonly offered. No more intolerable injury could be done to God than this because, as Bernard says, in making these offerings we attempt to transform God's gifts into our own glory: '. . . the more blest [we are] the more cursed if we make His graces our own glory without imputing all to him.'[19] Whatever we claim to be ours and then offer up in praise, we have actually stolen from God. God's generosity in providing such abundance to us only aggravates the crime of our sacrilege.

Knowing how prone we are to this sort of ingratitude, God tempers the means He uses to do good for us in ways hard for us to grasp. Thus, while He provided Gideon with an army, He didn't give him many soldiers.[20] While none of God's promises ever fail, they are accomplished in such a manner that, if we consider the circuit taken by the steps of His providence, we will be astonished along with the blessed Apostle who said, 'O the depth of the riches of the wisdom of God, how unsearchable are his counsels and his ways past finding out.'[21] Let it therefore always content us to take His word as an absolute warrant that we shall receive and find in the end. It shall be opened unto you. How? Where? By what means? Leave all that up to God.

— *God's Wonderful Providence* —

Our Lord bases each of our individual assurances on this point on the general rule and axiom of His providence which has ordained that the following results flow from these causes: from asking, gifts; from seeking, finding; from knocking, help. This is a principle so universally true that, for His part, it never fails. Why is this? Because it is the glory of God to give. His very nature delights in it. His mercy, flowing in the current through which we all pass, may seem dried up along the way but at the end it never fails.

We are soon weary both of granting and hearing petitions because our own inadequacies make us fearful lest by benefiting others we may impoverish ourselves. We read about the great largess that princes in their generous and vainglorious moods have poured forth – for example, that of Herod or of Ahasuerus in the Book of Esther, 'Ask what you will though it amount to half my kingdom, and I will give it to you.'[22] The very profusion of such words demonstrates that the ocean of no estate in the world may flow continuously without becoming empty.

He that promises half his kingdom foresees that when that is gone, the remainder is only half of what was. What we give, we lose. But what God bestows benefits us and takes nothing from Him. Thus, there are no fearful restraints in His propositions. His terms are general concerning the gift, 'whatever you ask the Father in my name', and general concerning who is affected, 'whoever asks, whoever seeks'.[23]

It is true, of course, that, as St James says, 'You ask and yet receive not because you ask wrongly. You crave what satisfies your own lusts.'[24] The rich man sought heaven but it was then that he fell into hell. The virgins knocked in vain because they missed their opportunity and when the time came to knock they were asleep. We must perform our duties to God in the appropriate time and manner.

Let us never stop seeking God. We may be sure that His bounty will be endless, above and beyond our desires. Saul sought an ass and found a kingdom. Solomon named wisdom and God gave him wealth also. 'You have overwhelmed your servant with blessings,' said the prophet David. 'He asked for life and you gave him long life, even eternal life.'[25]

God is a giver! 'He gives liberally and reproaches no one in any way.'[26] He knows better than we do the best times and the best means and the best things to give us for the good of our souls.

NOTES

1. Known traditionally as 'A Sermon Found in the Study of the Late Learned Bishop Andrewes', or 'A Sermon on Matthew 7.7'.
2. See W. Speed Hill, gen. ed., *The Folger Library Edition of the Works of Richard Hooker* Vols I–V (The Belknap Press of Harvard University, Cambridge, MA and London, 1977–1990), V, 379–84.

3. Psalms 119.76; 22.9.
4. Matthew 7.7–8.
5. Psalms 50.15; Proverbs 23.26.
6. Matthew 15.21–28; Luke 18.2–8; 1.52–53.
7. Hooker combines several scriptural references in Luke and Matthew to recount Christ's linking of tax collectors (publicans) and sinners and His preference for such of them who repent and follow Him to the leaders of the Temple who reject Him.
8. James 1.5; Proverbs 2.2, 4; 3.13; 16.16.
9. Matthew 19.16–17.
10. 2 Timothy 3.7.
11. 'From love they do not seek.' Bernard of Clairvaux actually said, 'Love does not seek her own'. For citation and comment see *Folger Edition*, V, 838–9.
12. Acts 2.37.
13. Song of Solomon 3.1.
14. Exodus 5.7–21; 14.5–9; 3.8, 17.
15. Genesis 49.14–15.
16. John 1.29.
17. Psalms 116.4, 6–8.
18. John 21.22.
19. Bernard, Abbot of Clairvaux, '*Sermones super Cantia Canticorum*', *Opera*, 1547, f.185r.
20. Judges 7.2–23.
21. Romans 11.33.
22. Esther 7.2.
23. Mark 6.22–23; John 16.23.
24. James 4.3.
25. Psalms 21.3–4.
26. James 1.5.

— 10 —
Faith and Works: Salvation for Roman Catholics[1]

When we last held St Paul's Epistle to the Hebrews in our hands, I read these words: 'In these last days he has spoken to us through his Son.'[2] I took that occasion to define the nature of the visible Church of Christ as a community of people sanctified through their profession of that truth that God taught the world through His Son. I declared that the whole scope of Christian doctrine is to comfort those who are overwrought with the burden of sin and I affirmed that the doctrine professed in the Church of Rome actually deprives men of comfort, both in their lives and at the time of their deaths. The conclusion I came to from all of this was that since the Church of Rome is as corrupted in faith as it is, refusing to be reformed, as it does, we must sever ourselves from it. Even the example of our fathers in the Roman Church may not keep us in communion and fellowship with that Church in the hope that by so doing we and they might be saved.

I do not doubt that God was merciful to save thousands of them, although they lived in popish superstition, because they sinned out of ignorance.[3] I ask you to mark and sift, with the strict severity of austere judgement, this last sentence of mine: 'God, I doubt not, was merciful to save thousands of our fathers living in popish superstition, in as much as they sinned out of ignorance.' This statement may be as good as gold and so a precious foundation for our beliefs. I protest that if what I have said proves to be nothing but hay or stubble, my own hand will set fire to it!

— *All Catholics are Not Damned* —

Two questions have arisen because of my earlier sermon on this subject: one, whether our fathers thus infected with popish errors and superstition might be saved; the other, whether their ignorance is a reasonable inducement to make us think that they might be. We will now examine, first what possibility, and then, what probability there is that God might be merciful to so many of our forefathers.

Some say that it could not be that our fathers living in popish superstition might be saved by the mercy of God because God has already spoken through His angel concerning Babylon (by which we may understand, the Church of Rome), saying, 'Go out of her my people lest you be partakers of her sins and receive her punishments.' In answer to this I say firstly, that these words referred only to temporal plagues, sorrows of death, famine, and fire with which God in His wrath had condemned Babylon. To save His chosen people [Israel] He said, 'Go out.' In the same way, God said in the Gospel, 'Let them that are in Judea fly into the mountains . . .' Similarly, in ancient times God said to Lot, 'Arise and take your wife and daughters who are here lest they be destroyed in the punishment of the city.'

But in this case God said, 'Go out of Babylon so that you will not be partakers of her sins or the resulting plagues upon her.' Since eternal and not temporal plagues are the punishment coming to Babylon, what is implied in God's statement is the everlasting destruction of Babylon and her inhabitants.[4]

How then can it be that so many of our forefathers in the Roman Church can be saved? Not only did they never depart from Babylon (the Roman Church) but they took her as their mother and died in her bosom. Well, in the first place we don't know what there might have been in common between our ancestors in this Church and the Babylonians. We do know that the people of Babylon were guilty of impieties and evils that they well understood and to which they gave their assent and which they could have avoided by leaving Babylon. Conversely, many members of the Church of Rome were guilty of very different sorts of sin, such as maintaining that the same credit and reverence that we give to the Scriptures of God ought to be given to unwritten truths, that the Pope is the supreme head of the universal Church, that the bread in the Eucharist is transubstantiated into Christ and is to be adored and offered up to God as a sacrifice for the quick and the dead, that images are to be worshipped, that Saints are to be called upon as intercessors, and such like.

— *Degrees and Kinds of Heresy* —

Some heresies concern matters of belief, such as the transubstantiation of sacramental elements in the Eucharist. Others concern matters of practice, such as the adoration of the elements. It is important to note that sometimes the practice is followed without any belief in the supporting doctrine. It is true that all who partake in the practical maintenance of heresy by word or deed participate in heresy. This is true both of those who are unaware that they are performing heretical acts and those who knowingly commit heresy. Those most in danger are people who commit and allow such acts when in their hearts and minds they condemn them.

Without doubt heresy is heretically maintained by those who obstinately hold and practise a heretical opinion after they have been properly admonished not to do so. I have no doubt that such people, along with another sort that I will identify in a moment, are inevitably condemned – unless they repent.

Lest anyone think that I am speaking of all of our Roman forefathers indifferently, I beseech you to mark my words carefully. What I am saying is that I do not doubt that God was merciful and did save *thousands* of our fathers in the Church of Rome. With God's help I will now set out plainly why I think this is so.

Many are partakers of the errors of the Church of Rome who are not implicated in its heresies. These people, following the conduct of their guides [priests] in the Church and doing exactly what was prescribed for them, thought they were doing God good service, when indeed they were dishonouring Him. This was their error. As for the heresies of the Roman Church, those dogmatic positions contrary to Christian truth, what one person among ten thousand in that Church ever understood them?

Even among those who understood the Roman heresies and allowed them to be practised all were not alike. Some, like the Popes and members of the Church Councils, were the founders and authors of heresy. This crime is one of which the people in the Church at large are generally free and clear. Among those who were receivers rather than authors of the Pope's heresies, not everyone was a master teacher. Many were merely intermediaries and teachers. Even those who sinned by teaching heresy did not teach all of the popish heresies. As St Jude says, 'Have compassion upon some.'[5]

Shall we lap them all up in one condition? Shall we cast them all without distinction headlong into the pit? Shall we plunge them all into that infernal and ever-flaming lake – those who have been merely participants in maintaining the error of Babylon along with those who have committed heretical acts, those who were the authors of heresy along with those who, by terror and violence, were forced to receive it, those who have taught heresy along with those simple folk who were seduced to believe error by the rhetorical tricks of false teachers, those who partook of one heresy along with those who partook of many, those of many along with those of all?

Notwithstanding that we find the condemnation of some of our forebears in the Church of Rome more tolerable than that of others, they are all, without exception, from the man who laboured at the plough to the man who sits in the Vatican – though some of them did but in ignorance practise the heresies they were taught – partakers of these heretical practices and beliefs and deserve the worldly punishments they receive for their sins. The pit of hell is usually the ending of the blind guide and those he guides alike.

But woe is the hour wherein we were born unless we can persuade ourselves of better endings, of salvation, even when we know that condemnation is due. We must show some way that our unwittingly sinful forefathers might escape eternal damnation. There is but one way and that is by appealing to the seat of God's saving mercy. (With Origen, we do not extend this mercy to devils and damned spirits, but we do say that God has mercy upon thousands even though there are thousands more whom He has condemned.) Christ has set the boundaries and fixed the limits of His saving mercy by two conditions. In chapter 3 of St John's Gospel we read that 'God did not send his Son to condemn the world but that through Him it might be saved. He that believes shall not be condemned. He that does not believe is condemned already. . .' In the second chapter of Revelation we read that mercy was denied to Jezebel because she did not repent.[6] Therefore, our hope for our fathers in the Church of Rome is in vain if they were altogether faithless and unrepentant.

Those who were either weak in assenting to Christian truth or stubborn in maintaining ideas that in some ways were opposed to true doctrine were not entirely faithless. All who held fast to the most precious foundations of true faith, even if they did so weakly, as it were, by a slender thread and even if they built many base and unsuitable ideas on that thread, ideas that cannot withstand the trial of the fire, yet they shall pass through the fire and be saved, so long as they have built themselves upon the rock which is the foundation of the Church. If our fathers did not hold on to this foundation, there is no doubt they were faithless. If many of them held to it then there is no necessary impediment to their salvation. Let us then see what the foundation of faith is and whether or not we may think that thousands of our fathers living in popish superstition, notwithstanding, held to that foundation.

— *The Foundation of Faith* —

If the foundation of the faith imports the general ground wherein we rest our beliefs, then the writings of the Evangelists and Apostles are the foundation of Christian faith. O, that the Church of Rome as soundly interpreted these fundamental writings as it willingly holds and embraces them. If the word 'foundation' denotes the principal thing believed, then we find it in what St Paul said to Timothy, 'God manifested in the flesh, justified in the spirit, etc.,' or the words of Nathaniel, 'Thou art the Son of the living God. Thou art the king of Israel,' or the words of the people of Samaria, 'This is Christ, the Saviour of the world.'[7] Whoever directly denies these words utterly uproots the very foundation of our faith.

I have shown earlier that, although the Church of Rome has played the harlot worse than Israel ever did, yet they are not, as are the Jewish synagogues which plainly deny Christ, clearly and cleanly excluded from the new covenant. Whatsoever we term the Church of Rome, when we compare her to reformed churches, we make a distinction between Rome and heathenish assemblies. However, I grant that the Church of Rome and all her children are excluded from salvation and are no better than Saracen Turks if they directly deny that Christ was crucified for the salvation of the world.

Do we know how many millions of our fathers in the Roman Church may have ended their mortal lives by uttering, before their breath ceased, these words of faith: 'Christ, my Saviour, my Redeemer, Jesus'? Shall we say of them that they did not hold the foundation of Christian faith?

Answer is made by some that these Romans might sincerely confess Jesus as Saviour and yet be far from salvation. As the Apostle Paul said, 'I say unto you that if you be circumcised Christ shall profit you nothing.' Christ alone, they say, is the means of our salvation. Like the Galatians, who add the work of circumcision and other rites to Christ's law, these people are cast away from salvation. The Church of Rome, they say, also teaches her children to join other things to Christ's law. Therefore, their faith profits them nothing at all.[8]

It is true that Rome did indeed add other things to faith in Christ. But how? Not in the work of redemption itself, which the Romanists grant that Christ alone performed sufficiently for the salvation of the whole world. It is only in the *application* of this inestimable treasure that they make additions, so that Christ might be an effectual instrument of salvation. Here, despite their coy claim that they seek remission of sins by no other means than Christ's blood and are only humbly using the means approved by Him to secure the benefit of His blood, they in fact teach so many things pernicious to Christian faith that the very foundation of the faith which they hold is plainly overthrown and the power of the blood of Jesus Christ extinguished. We are right, therefore, to dispute with them, press them, urge them, using even the dire consequences which the Apostle used with the Galatians.

I insist that if some of those Galatians, heartily embracing the Gospel of Christ, were sincere and sound in faith, except for this one error [circumcision], and ended their lives before they had been taught that their opinion was perilous, we should not think that the damage of this error would so outweigh the benefit of their faith that the mercy of God might not save them.

— *Lutheran Heresies?* —

I grant that in some consequent fashion the Galatians overthrew the foundation of faith but so do the Lutheran churches which in our own day stiffly and fiercely maintain a false doctrine from the heretic Nestor, regarding the nature of Christ [that He is God and man in two separate beings] and taught by Luther himself. That this heresy of Nestor's overthrows the foundation of faith no one not committing it will deny. Luther's version of the heresy is not a direct denial of the foundation but it may be regarded as damnable by some. I think that in many respects it is less forgivable today in the form that Luther and others hold it than it was originally.[9]

But the question is not whether an error is made but whether that mistake excludes the possibility of salvation unless it is expressly recanted and repented of. For my part, I dare not deny the possibility of salvation for the Lutherans when they have been a chief instrument of our own redemption, even if they do carry to their graves a doctrine which is greatly repugnant to the truth.

Therefore, in so far as it may be said that the Church of Rome still has a little of the strength of truth left, that is because she does not directly deny the foundation of Christianity. I may, I trust, without offence, persuade myself that thousands of our fathers in former times, living and dying within her walls, have found mercy at the hands of God.

Even if they did not repent their errors in doctrine, you ask? God forbid that I should open my mouth to deny that which Christ said, 'Except you repent, you shall all perish.'[10] And if they did not repent, then they perished. Yet how many things escape our notice when we have no knowledge of them? How many of these might be sins? Without knowledge and awareness of sin, there can be no repentance.

We can only choose to conclude that, for all who held fast to their basic faith and hated all of their unknown sins and errors, the blessing of repentance is obtained at the hands of God through the gracious mediation of Christ Jesus, so long as they uttered a cry, with the prophet David, 'Purge me, O Lord, from my secret [unknown] sins.'[11]

But we wash a wall of loam, we labour in vain, our argument goes for nothing if we apply it to those who directly deny the foundation of Christian faith. Even infidels and heathens are not so godless as not to cry to God for a general mercy for forgiveness of their sins. To them and others who deny faith there can be no salvation in the ordinary manner which God uses to save us without our repenting of our particular sins. The Galatians, in thinking that unless they were circumcised they could not be saved, directly overthrew the foundation of faith. If any of them died holding that persuasion, their situation is dreadful – for there is nothing for them but death and condemnation.

The same is true for many in the Church of Rome. Did not St Paul speak about how the Antichrist would seduce the Romanists long before it happened? As he said, 'They received not the love of truth that could save them and therefore God would send them strange delusions inducing them to believe lies; thus all might be damned who did not believe the truth but took pleasure in unrighteousness.' As St John said, 'All that dwell upon earth whose names are not written in the Book of Life shall worship him.'[12]

Many in former times, as their books and writings show, held to the foundation of faith, to whit, that salvation is by Christ alone. These people may be saved. God has always had a Church among those who firmly keep His saving truth. Those who hold with the Church of Rome that we cannot be saved without works have not the saving truth of Christ, no not even by so much as a slender thread.

To the best of my memory, I am addressing all the reasonable arguments against my earlier statements on this subject and hope that if one final question is answered the controversy will end. That concerns my idea that a general repentance might suffice for our sinning fathers in the Church of Rome. I am asked whether a murderer or blasphemer or unclean Turk or Jew or any sinner can escape the wrath of God by a simple, 'God, forgive me.' Certainly, I have never entertained in my heart the belief that such a general repentance would serve for all sins and for all sinners. This sort of repentance is applicable only as a common oversight of our sinful lives and for faults which either escaped our notice or which we did not know were faults.

Unless our fathers in the Church of Rome were actually penitent of sins wherein they knowingly displeased God, they are not to be included within my argument for their possible salvation. Unless they held to the foundation of faith, I have both affirmed and proved that they could not be saved. Yet I have asked, 'Is it not possible that thousands of our fathers, though they lived in popish superstition, might yet be saved by God's mercy?'

In the first place, if our forefathers directly denied the foundation of faith without repenting of their particular sins, whoever says there is no salvation for them by the ordinary means God uses to save us is implying that God might deliver them from hell by some extraordinary extension of mercy. Secondly, granted that the foundation is denied by some heresy fostered by the Church of Rome, I ask how many there are who, being seduced by the common errors of the Church of Rome, never understood the meaning of the Church's heresies? If all the papist heretics perished, surely thousands who only lived in popish superstition might be saved. Thirdly, since all who held some popish heresies did not hold all of them, why might not thousands who were infected with other [better] leaven live or die unsoured by heresy, and thus be saved? Fourthly, there may no doubt be many who held a given heresy only in a general verbal sense which might have been expounded to them in a way too far removed from doctrinal heresy to poison them. For example, think of those who held that we cannot be saved by Christ without good works. We ourselves (I think) say as much. To be sure, except for infants or persons who die at the point of conversion to the faith, none will see God unless they seek peace and holiness. Such seeking is not the cause of their salvation but it is a path which must be walked by those who would be saved. If anyone holds that without works we are not justified and if they imply sanctification within their meaning of justification, St James said as much.

— *Faith, Works, Righteousness and Justification* —

Unless there is some ambiguity in these words [salvation, righteousness, justification and sanctification], St Paul and St James seem to contradict one another on the issue of faith and works. This cannot be. What we discover is that justification for Paul does not imply sanctification when he says that we are justified by faith without works. Justification does sometimes imply sanctification for St James. So there are two kinds of righteousness, one which is imputed to us by God and one which consists of our works of faith, hope, charity and other Christian virtues.[13]

The results of this sanctifying righteousness are the fruits and the operations [works] of the faithful spirit. The distinction here is between *habitual* and *actual* righteousness. *Habitual* is that with which souls are inwardly endowed from the time when we first became the temples of the Holy Ghost. *Actual* is that holiness for which Enoch, Job, Zachary, Elizabeth, and other Saints in Scripture are so highly commended.[14]

If you demand to know which of these two kinds of justification we received first, I answer that it is the habitual justice which is first engrafted in, or imputed to, us. Actual righteousness, which comes through good works, comes afterwards both in order of importance and in time. When we attentively study this matter we see clearly that the faith of true believers cannot be divorced from love and hope, that faith is a part of sanctification, that faith is perfected by good works, and that no work of ours is good without faith.

In this sense, we can understand how our fathers in the Church of Rome might hold that we are justified by faith alone and at the same time hold, correctly, that without good works, we are not justified.

Did they also think that we earn rewards in heaven by the works we perform on earth? Clearly, the ancient Fathers connected merit with obtaining salvation. In this same sense, the Lutherans, in their *Wittenberg Confession*, say, 'We teach that good works commanded of God are necessary and that by the free mercy of God they earn their own rewards, either corporal or spiritual.'[15]

When others [Lutherans] speak as our Roman forefathers did, we take their meaning to be sound. Charity requires that, since our forefathers' meaning is uncertain, we should give a favourable rather than an unfavourable construction to their words as well. Even if we accept the worst construction, namely that *all* embraced the false doctrine while alive, might not we suppose that many of them renounced the heresy at the time of their death?

After all, when people feel easy about themselves, they vainly tickle their fancies with who knows what reckless ideas about the connection between their merits and their rewards, which, in the trance of their high speculations, they dream God has weighed up and laid out, as it were, in bundles for them. Nevertheless, we see by daily experience that some people, as the hour of death approaches, as they hear themselves summoned to appear and stand at the bar of the Judge whose brightness causes the eyes of the angels themselves to be dazzled, begin to hide the faces of their idle imaginations. To name their merits at such a time is to lay their souls upon the rack. The memory of their deeds is then loathsome to them. They forsake everything in which they had previously put their trust and confidence. There is no staff to lean upon, no ease, no rest, no comfort then, except in Christ Jesus.

But what if it is not true at all that neither the Galatians, with their circumcision, nor this Church of Rome, with its required works, are, after all, in any direct denial of the foundation of faith, as is so often affirmed? I need not wade too far into this controversy which I trust is now clarified. However, since I wish the truth in this matter to be fully illumined, I will do my best to set down my beliefs even more plainly: first, as to what the foundation of faith is; second, what it means to deny the foundation; third, whether those whom God has chosen to be His heirs of life everlasting may fall so far as directly to deny His will; fourth, whether the Galatians did just that by committing the error over circumcision; last, whether the Church of Rome, because of this one opinion concerning the importance of works, may also be thought to have fallen and therefore to be no more a Christian Church than are the assemblies of Turks and Jews.

— *The Foundation Explored More Fully* —

This word 'foundation' when used figuratively always refers to something which resembles an actual building as, in this case, both the basic Christian doctrine and the living communities of Christian people do. Students of public policy have taught consistently that commonwealths are founded upon laws and that only by a general acceptance of these laws, which keep them in order, can a multitude be formed into a single body politic. The ground of all civil law is this: *No one ought to be hurt or injured by another*. Take away this agreement and you take away all laws; take away all laws and what becomes of commonwealths?

So it is with our spiritual Christian community. I do not refer here to that mystical body whereof Christ is the only head – the building that is invisible to mortal eyes, wherein Christ is the chief cornerstone. I speak rather of the visible Church, the foundation of which is the doctrine professed by the Prophets and the Apostles. The goal toward which their doctrine points is expressed in the words of St Peter to Christ when he says, 'You have the words of eternal life', or in the words of St Paul to Timothy, 'The Holy Scriptures are able to make you wise about salvation.'[16] This desire for immortality and for the knowledge of how to attain it is so natural to all people that even those who are not sure what to do with their lives wish to know how to avoid an end to life. And because there are no natural means yet devised to resist the face of death, we won't find any people on earth so primitive that they haven't devised some supernatural power or other to fly to for aid and succour when threatened by their mortal enemies.

This longing to be saved, without understanding the true way to do it, has been the cause of all the superstitions in the world. O, that the miserable state of those who wander in darkness and know not where they are going could give us understanding hearts worthy of esteeming God's mercy towards us, before whose eyes He has the doors of the kingdom of heaven set wide open. Should we not offer violence to the darkness of ignorance? It offers violence to us even as we gather the strength of our faith to withstand it.

But I digress when I pause to bewail the coldness which we bear toward the very grace that would save us. My purpose is only to set forth the ground of our salvation, which it is the sole end of the Gospel to propound. And does not the Gospel show us the path to salvation? Yes! 'The damsel possessed with the spirit of divination' spoke the truth when she said, 'These men are the servants of the most high God who shows us the way of salvation.'[17] This is what Paul, in Hebrews 10.20, calls 'a new and living way which Christ has prepared for us, through the valley that is His flesh' – salvation purchased by the death of Christ.

By this foundation the children of God, before the time of written law, were distinguished from the sons of men. The reverend Fathers of the Church professed this while living and at the hour of their death (Genesis 49). This faith comforted Job in the midst of his grief (Job 19). It was later the anchor of all the righteous in Israel, from the time of the written law to the time of God's grace in Christ. Every Prophet makes mention of it. This faith was so widely spoken of, by the time of Christ's coming to fulfil the promises made so long ago, that the sound of it was heard even among the Gentiles.

When Christ came all those who were His children acknowledged that He was their salvation – the long-expected hope of Israel, the seed in whom all the nations of the world would be blessed. But now His name is the name of ruin, death and condemnation to those who dream of new messiahs and look for salvation by any other means but Him. Yet Luke (2.30) says, 'Amongst men there is given no other name under heaven whereby we may be saved.' St Mark intimates the same truth in the words with which he begins his Book: 'The beginning of the Gospel of Jesus Christ, the Son of God.' He calls his writing a Gospel of Jesus Christ because it teaches the way to salvation through Christ.[18]

This then is the foundation on which the frame of the Gospel is erected. It is that same Jesus whom the Virgin conceived by the Holy Ghost, whom Simon Peter embraced in his arms, whom Pilate condemned, whom the Jews crucified, whom the Apostles preached – the Lord, the only Saviour of the world. We can lay down no other foundation but Him.

In brief form I have now set forth the principle of Christianity which we call the foundation of our faith. Now I will show you what it is to overthrow it. To make this as clear as possible we should first understand what it means to affirm and hold fast to the foundation of faith.

There are those who maintain that many of the Gentiles who never heard the name of Christ nevertheless held to the foundation of faith. Why? Because they acknowledged the sovereignty of God, His infinite wisdom, strength and power, His goodness and His mercy toward the children of men, and they believed that God has judgements in store for the wicked and rewards for the righteous, etc. In all this, some say, they join us in our beliefs. The foundation of our faith in Christ lies secretly wrapped up and contained in these rudiments of their knowledge about God. Therefore some allege that they held the foundation of faith, even though they never heard of it.

Might we not with as good a colour of reason defend the proposition that every ploughman has in his command all the sciences wherein the philosophers have excelled? For no one is ignorant of the first principles which virtually contain whatever either is or could be known by natural reason. With just such use of reason might we not affirm that a man might put three mighty oak trees wherever three acorns might be put, since an acorn is essentially an oak tree? To avoid just such paradoxes we teach plainly that the proof that one holds the faith must be that one acknowledges it expressly.

— *Overthrowing the Foundation of Faith* —

Because the foundation of faith is a direct affirmative, all those who deny it directly overthrow it. Also, those who hold to a proposition whose consequence is an indirect denial of faith are overthrowing the foundation. What is the question between us and the Gentiles and Jews but this: whether salvation comes by Christ; whether salvation comes by this Jesus – yes or no? This is the main point whereupon Christianity stands. Paul makes this clear in a sentence spoken by Festus regarding Paul's accusers: 'They [. . .] had certain questions against him and one question of Jesus who had died and whom Paul said was alive.' From this we see that the Jews and the Gentiles despised and a Christian Apostle maintained the belief that Jesus died and was raised for the salvation of the world. In the same manner the Fathers in the early Church [. . .] stood in defence of Christianity against those who directly denied the foundation of faith. The later writings of the Fathers against the Novatians, Pelagians and other heretics refuted doctrines wherein the foundation of faith was indirectly overthrown.[19]

All infidels, therefore, have denied the foundation of faith directly. By consequent or indirect denials, many a Christian, indeed whole Christian churches, have also done so and continue in such denials at this present day. When Christian churches deny the faith directly they cease to be Christian churches, but when only indirectly, we condemn them for being in error but still hold them to be Christian for upholding the basic foundation of faith.

We see now what it is to hold the foundation and what it is to deny it both directly and indirectly. What follows next in our inquiry is to examine whether those whom God has chosen may afterwards fall so far as to deny directly the foundation which their hearts had once embraced with joy and comfort in the Holy Christ.

Devils know that the minds of the ungodly may be fully persuaded of the truth of what we believe. Such knowledge is sometimes called faith. But this is equivocal, being no such faith as that whereby a Christian is justified. It is the spirit of God's adoption of us that instils faith in us – and not in them. What we believe, we have apprehended not only as true, but as good. By them is apprehended only the truth and not the goodness of the foundation of faith.

Whereupon follows a third difference between Christians and others. As the faith of the Christian increases so does his joy and comfort, whereas the more sure others are of the truth the more they quake and tremble at it. This produces another way in which the hearts of the two groups have different dispositions toward the truth they both perceive. The wicked often think that death would be preferable to God's punishment. For others (like us) there is no grief or torment greater than to feel that our faith is weak, because we reap such comfort and joy of spirit in our faith and this, in turn, is because the principal object of faith is that Jesus Christ is the only saviour of the world.

The very cause of the spiritual life in us is Christ, not as He inhabits us in some carnal or bodily sense, but as something dwelling in our souls which, when the mind apprehends it, is said to inhabit and possess the mind. The mind conceives of Christ by hearing Christian doctrine. Even as the light of nature causes the mind to grasp those truths which are merely rational, so the saving truth, which is far above the reach of human reason, cannot be conceived except through the operation of the spirit of the Almighty.

Whenever we read such words as, 'the Spirit is our life', or 'Christ is our life,' we are to understand that our life is Christ, through the hearing of the Gospel and then believing, through the power of the Holy Ghost. The first intellectual comprehension of Christ so embraced St Peter that he called it 'the seed whereby we are born anew'. Our own first embracing of Christ is our first rebirth from the state of death and condemnation. 'He that has the Son, has life; and, he that has not the Son of God, has not life,' says St John. If, therefore, he who once had the Son ceases to have Him, though only for a moment, he ceases to have life itself. The lives of those who live by the Son of God are everlasting, not only in the life hereafter. Being always alive to God in Jesus Christ, they live for ever from the time of their justification.

If I had not already done so, I could show you by various obvious proofs how the motions and operations of life are sometimes so invisible and secret that people seem stone dead who are actually still alive to God in Christ. For so long as that which abides in us animates, quickens, and gives life to us, we remain alive. We know that the very cause of our lives abides within us for ever. If Christ, the foundation of life, may flit away and leave the habitation where He once dwelt, what would become of His promise, 'I am with you to the world's end'? If the seed of God, which contains Christ, may first be conceived and then cast out, how can St Peter call that seed 'immortal' or St John say that 'it abideth'?[20]

If, therefore, we who were once justified by faith live by faith for ever, it follows that we who once believed in the foundation of faith do so for ever. And if we do, can we ever directly deny that faith?

You will say that one who is holy today may forsake holiness and become impure tomorrow. As a friend may change his mind and become an enemy, as hope may wither, so faith may die in the heart of anyone, as the Spirit is quenched and grace extinguished, so those who once believed may be turned quite away from the truth. To you, all of this seems obvious, proved by long experience.

— *The Power of Repentance* —

I grant that we are ever ready to forsake God. But is God as ready to forsake us? Because our minds are so changeable, is His? Has not Christ assured us that whosoever God has justified, He will give a kingdom so long as they remain grounded in the faith, do not abandon the hope promised in the Gospel, and abide in love and holiness? When our Saviour spoke of the sheep who had been called and gathered into His fold, He said, 'I give unto them eternal life and they shall never perish, neither shall anyone pluck them out of my hands.'[21] Without doubt, in so saying He was promising to preserve them not only in that faith without which there is no salvation, but also from anything that would cause an irremediable loss of salvation.

Truly, every error in our ideas about God is repugnant to our faith, just as every fearful thought is repugnant to hope, as every roaming, inordinate desire to love, as every blemish in our lives, is to holiness. By such inward thoughts and outward deeds our lives are stained. [. . .] But even infidelity, extreme despair, hatred of God and all godliness, or stubbornness in sin, cannot prevail if there is but the smallest spark of faith, hope, love or holiness in us – even as the lowest degree of cold is not reached so long as there is one degree of heat remaining.

Whereupon I conclude that no one lives who does not sin – not even the most seemingly perfect. Yet the person who is chosen by God has a promise that within him the seed of God shall abide, a seed that is a guaranteed preservation against sin. We cannot have greater or clearer assurances of anything than of this – God will preserve the righteous, the apple of His eye, from sin for ever. Hence a person who has once sincerely believed in Christ cannot directly deny the grounding of his faith.

But, you ask, did not Peter, Marcellus,[22] and many others directly deny Christ after they had first believed, and yet believed again after they had denied Him? No, because, unlike Judas, they never ceased inwardly to remain faithful to Christ in their hearts even though they failed to repent. Still, because they sinned so notoriously and grievously in denying Christ, it was necessary that Christ, Who had intended to save them, touch their hearts with true repentance. In this way His mercy might restore them to life.

I hope that I may safely say that if a person whom God has justified errs, as he may, and never comes to understand his error, God will save him if he participates in a general repentance. But if such a person commits heresy, he must make an act of specific penance. If he is unfaithful by a direct inward denial of the foundation, God, by His special providence, still preserves him and all those He has justified for ever. Thus we know what to think of those Galatians whose hearts had been at one time so possessed of love of God's truth, 'that, if it had been possible, they would have plucked out their very eyes' to bestow upon their teachers. Later on, it is true, they changed their persuasion and affection so that, by the time St Paul wrote to them, they had strayed through error. This I do not deny but I do deny that, if they were indeed His sheep, they were damned when they erred out of ignorance.

— *The Case of the Galatians* —

We must make a distinction between those who stray from God out of ignorance of the truth but retain a mind desirous of being instructed, and those who persist in stubborn defence of their blindness even after the truth is laid open to them.

These heretical defenders, these forward and stiff-necked teachers of circumcision, the Apostle called 'dogs'. These simple men, who were seduced to think they taught the truth, the Apostle pitied, took up into his arms, lovingly embraced and kissed. Then, with more than fatherly tenderness to temper and qualify his harsh words, the Apostle makes it difficult for us to discern whether he was filled more with love for their godliness or grief for the danger inherent in their dangerous opinion on circumcision.[23] Their opinion was dangerous, but was not also the opinion of those who thought that the kingdom of Christ would be earthly, or those who taught that the Gospel should be preached only to the Jews? (What could be more opposed to the Prophets concerning Christ's coming than the one and what more opposed to the Catholic Church than the other?) Yet when these teachers and their followers held these fantasies they were not the worst men in the world. Yes, the heresy of free will was a millstone about the neck of the Pelagians but shall we therefore pronounce sentence of inevitable damnation upon all those of our ancestors in the Greek Church who were misled into believing this erroneous doctrine of free will?[24] Of those Galatians, therefore, who were first justified and later deceived by error, I see no reason why they may not have been saved by God's mercy so long as they returned to the truth when they were admonished to do so. About this, I take it, there is no disagreement. Only against the salvation of those who died before they were admonished to abandon their error is it objected that the Galatians' false opinion amounts to a very clear and direct denial of the foundation of faith.

Lest I should seem here to hold an opinion that no godly or learned person has ever held, let the following words be taken to explain what I am affirming: those brethren who in St Paul's day thought God required them to obey certain rules about holy days and what foods they could eat could not help but condemn a freedom from the law of God, which freedom they supposed, however erroneously, was being advocated contrary to divine Scripture. [. . .] Their error, if you weigh what it really is, was to refute the entire Scripture, which teaches that salvation comes through faith in Christ, or all that the Prophets foretold, or all that the Apostles taught about Christ. Their error, which implied a complete denial of Christ, led St Paul to complain that his labour among them was in vain. St Paul complained that his labour among them was fruitless because their practice of circumcision would profit them nothing at all. Yet, so far was St Paul from striking their names out of Christ's book that he commanded others to entertain them, to accept their singular humanity, to treat them like brothers. St Paul understood our weakness, had a feeling for the great blindness of us mortals, and retained his certainty that we are the sons of God for so long as we are endowed with His love. Paul would not count the Galatians as enemies of a truth they could not yet accept as long as they persisted in their unwitting rejection of and resistance to the faith. In the midst of it all, the Galatians continued to acknowledge Christ as their only and perfect Saviour, not seeing how repugnant their belief in the necessity of Mosaical ceremonies was to their faith in Christ.

It may be replied to my argument that, if the Galatians had not directly denied the foundation, they might have been saved. But, as it is, they cannot be saved because their denial was not indirect (by consequent belief or action) but direct. When the question concerned the possibility of their salvation, the matter of their denial of the foundation was brought forth as proof that they could not be saved. Now that the question is about their denial of the foundation, the impossibility of their salvation is alleged to prove that they denied the foundation.

Is there nothing that can exclude people from salvation except denial of the foundation of faith? I should have thought that many other beliefs and actions might lead to eternal death, unless they were repented of, just as this opinion of the Galatians about circumcision was death for those who came to understand that, if they persisted in this error, they would fall from Christ's grace but, notwithstanding, held on to their mistake.

But enough of all this!

— *Rome Does Not Overthrow the Faith* —

I come now to the last question: whether the doctrines of the Church of Rome concerning the necessity of works for salvation is a direct denial of the foundation of our faith.

I do not seek here to impose upon you any private opinion of my own, for the most learned opinions of our profession hold that all the heresies and corruptions of the Church of Rome do not prove that it directly denied the foundation of faith. If that had been proved, then that church would simply be no Christian Church at all. Calvin said that in the papal church something of the true

Church does remain, a church crazed, if you will, broken quite into pieces, forlorn, misshapen, yet still a church. Calvin's reasoning was that, before faith is utterly denied, the Antichrist must 'sit in the Temple of God'.

Lest anyone think that salvation applies only to those whom God, in His providence, is supposed to have kept free from imperfection and as sound in the faith as we trust, by God's mercy, that we are, I submit the following for your wise consideration. Is it not likely that, even as emotion can take away the use of reason and yet proves that those who are emotional are reasonable because they choose to display their emotions, so antichristianity, being the bane and overthrow of Christianity, may nevertheless demonstrate that the church where the Antichrist sits is a Christian church?

I have not heard or read any authoritative argument that God [. . .] fails to keep His elect from 'worshipping the beast' [the Antichrist] and receiving his mark on their foreheads. Rather, He has preserved and will preserve them from receiving any deadly wound at the hands of the man of sin [the Pope], whose deceits have prevailed over no one except those who never loved the truth and took pleasure in their unrighteousness. Those, in all ages, whose hearts have delighted in Christ and whose souls have thirsted after righteousness, even though they erred dangerously, might be saved by God's mercy. Even if they were marked by heresy, I do not doubt that God's mercy will convert them.

How far Romish heresies may prevail over God's elect, how many people God has kept from falling into these heresies, how many have been converted from them, is not the question here. Even if heaven had not accepted any one person of the Romish stamp for a thousand years, it may still be true that the doctrine which is professed today does not directly deny the ground of faith and thus disprove that this is a Christian Church.

I have already cited authorities whose works support what I am saying here. There are others, one of whom says plainly that he could no more deny the name of 'Christian Church' to the Roman Church than he could deny the name of man to a person, so long as he lives, no matter what sickness he has. The reasoning for this opinion is that, despite all the wickedness of the Pope in pardoning wicked deeds and in emphasizing the merits of the Saints, the life of the Roman Church holds on, if only by a very thin thread. Another author, Jerome Zanchius of Bergamo has said, 'I acknowledge the Church of Rome even in this present day to be a church of Christ, like the church of Israel under Jeroboam, but still a church.' His reasoning was that:

> Every man sees, unless he willingly hoodwinks himself, that, now as in the past, the Church of Rome holds firmly and steadfastly to the truth concerning our Lord Jesus Christ, baptizes in the name of the Father, the Son, and the holy Ghost, confesses Christ as the only redeemer of the world and the judge who will [. . .] receive true believers into endless joy – faithless and godless men being cast with Satan and his angels into unquenchable flames.[25]

I will rein in this discussion shorter than other authorities have done. Let the Pope take off his tiara and captivate no more souls by his power. Let him no longer count himself as chief lord over the princes of the world and no longer hold kings as his tenants. Let his stately Senate submit their necks to the yoke of Christ and cease to dye their garments in blood. Let them, from the highest to the lowest, hate and forsake their idolatry, abjure all the errors and heresies with which they have perverted the truth. Let them strip their church until they leave no polluted rag and retain only this one absolute falsehood – that we cannot be saved by Christ without our good works. It will be sufficient now if I can show that the holding of this one false doctrine does not prove that the foundation of faith has been directly denied by the Church of Rome.

— *Works and Faith* —

Works are an addition to the foundation of our faith. So be it. What then? Surely the foundation is not subverted by every addition to it. Simply to add to fundamental faith in Christ is not necessarily to mingle wine with dirty water, heaven with earth, things polluted with the sanctified blood of Christ. [. . .] And if I now open my mouth to speak in defence of the Romanists or if I simply hold my peace and do not argue against them as long as there is breath in my body, let me be guilty of all the dishonour that has ever been done to the Son of God. It is such a dreadful thing to deny salvation by Christ alone that I am slow and fearful to lay so grievous a charge on any man. Let us beware lest we find so many ways of denying Christ that we ourselves can scarcely find a way to truly and soundly confess Him.

To be sure, the faith that salvation comes only from Christ is the true foundation upon which all of Christianity stands. But what if I say that you cannot be saved by Christ unless you add that Christ 'believed in his heart, confessed with his mouth and obeyed in his life and conversation'? Because I add this requirement, do I, therefore, deny that which I have directly affirmed? There may be additions to basic doctrine which do not overthrow but serve to prove or complete the proposition to which they are annexed. For example, he who says Peter was a *chief apostle* affirms that Peter was an Apostle, and he who says that our salvation is from the Lord *through sanctification of the spirit and faith in the truth* (2 Thessalonians 2.13) affirms that our salvation is from the Lord. On the other hand, if that which is added is such a diminution that it takes away the very essence of the proposition to which it is adjoined, then, by consequence, the proposition itself is overthrown.

He who says that Judas is a dead man grants that Judas is a man but at the same time says that he is not a man because death deprives him of his life. Similarly, he who says that our election by God is through His grace because of our works is denying that our election is by grace because the grace which elected us is not grace but grace caused by works.

Now whereas the Church of Rome adds works as a requirement for salvation, we must note that this is not the same as the Galatians adding circumcision. Christ did not come to abrogate and take away good works, but He did come to abolish circumcision, for He replaced it with holy Baptism. To say that you cannot be saved by

Christ unless you are circumcised is to add an act which Christ has prohibited, something not only unnecessary but necessary not to be performed by any who wished to be saved. On the other hand, to say that you cannot be saved without good works is to add a requirement that is not specifically excluded by Christ and is, in some instances, required as an important addition to faith by Christ Himself who spun the web of salvation. He said, 'unless your righteousness exceeds that of the scribes and Pharisees you will not enter the kingdom of heaven' (Matthew 5.20). [. . .] Works of righteousness, therefore, are not so repugnantly added to faith as circumcision is. We say that our salvation is by Christ alone and so whatever we add to this is overthrowing Christ. Our case would be difficult to prove if this argument were good and sound in the universal manner in which it is stated. But we do not teach Christ alone, apart from our act of faith, or Christ alone, apart from our works which are necessary for sanctification.

It is a childish cavil for our Roman adversaries to please themselves by exclaiming that we tread underfoot all Christian virtues and require nothing in Christians but faith because we teach that men are justified by faith alone. In fact we have never meant to exclude hope and charity as inseparable mates of faith in the person who is justified by faith, or, for that matter, to say that good works are not duties required at the hands of every justified man. We have meant only to demonstrate that faith is the only hand that cloaks us with the justification of Christ, the only garment which, once put on, covers the shame of our defiled natures, hides the imperfections of our works, and preserves us blameless in the sight of God, before whom the weakness of our faith is otherwise so insufficient as to make us guilty and to shut us out from the kingdom of heaven where nothing impure may enter.

So that our dealing with our foes will not be so childish as theirs is with us, let me explain that when we say salvation is wrought by Christ alone we understand that 'alone' is an exclusive adjective and that we need to explain exactly what is excluded and how. If I say that such and such a judge ought to hear such and such a case, I am not thereby excluding all others from assisting with such supporting matters as witnessing and giving depositions. Others are only excluded from making the decision and giving the sentence. How then is our salvation wrought by Christ alone?

Is it my meaning that nothing is required for salvation but Christ's silent action, without anything more to be done? No. We acknowledge no such doctrine. Rather I teach what I myself have been taught, namely that, in addition to that quiet, bare, naked work wherein Christ without any other associate purchased our salvation, the actual conveyance to us of this great blessing requires much more. It requires that we were known and chosen by God before the foundation of the world, justified in this life, and after our deaths, sanctified and received by God in heaven. There are some aspects of each of these separate works in which Christ has acted alone. Through Him who was crucified, buried, raised, etc., according to God's eternal purpose, before the foundation of the world, we were known by God long before we were seen by men. God knew us and was good to us in Christ Jesus. In Him we were elected to be heirs of eternal life.

To this point, God worked through Christ in such a way that we were mere patients, functioning as no more than any dead or senseless matter, no more than wood or stone or iron in the artificer's hand, or clay before it is formed by a potter to some honourable use – no, not even this much life in us because the craftsman chooses material which is suitable to his purpose and in us there is no such quality.

None of this means that we are not required to act also. Our vocation is to listen to the Gospel, express the fruits, or works, of the Spirit, and persevere in hope, faith, and holy living.

What then is the error of the Church of Rome? Not that it requires good works at the hands of those who would be saved but that it attributes to these works the power of satisfying God for our sins, and claims a virtue in us which earns God's grace here on earth and glory for us in heaven. That this indirectly overthrows the foundation of faith, I willingly grant. That it is a direct denial of Christ, I utterly deny. I have already explained what it means both to hold and to deny directly the foundation of faith. Apply that to this case and there need be no more ado about the issue. [. . .] Salvation by Christ is the foundation of Christianity. As for works, they are something subordinate; they are necessary only because our sanctification cannot be accomplished without them.

The doctrine of works is a subordinate doctrine that is built on to the foundation of faith. The idea that works have the power to satisfy God or earn salvation is an addition to an already subordinate doctrine and not to the foundation itself. Yet the foundation is, as a consequence, overthrown because through this addition it may be concluded that any who claim, as do papist priests, to convert our works into supposedly freely willed good works presented before the sight of God, or to invest our good works with the power to satisfy God's wrath for our sins, or to earn us heavenly or earthly rewards, or who indicate that our good works might facilitate our election to salvation and our justification through the process of sanctification, have pulled out our faith by its very roots.

From this comes plain and direct denial of the foundation. Not only this heresy but other consequent heresies raze the foundation of our faith. However much we try to differentiate heresies into varying degrees of infidelity caused by denying various articles of our faith, the inference can always be drawn that the foundation is thereby denied. For example, if someone should say there is no Catholic Church, it follows that Jesus, whom we call the Saviour, is not the saviour of the whole world because the Prophets bear witness that the true Messiah should 'show light to the Gentiles' (Acts 26.23). This is taken to mean a catholic church, one no longer limited to a circumcised nation.

Thus we place in a second rank those positions of a similar nature from which the denial of true doctrine *might be* concluded. These would include denials of Christ's divinity or of his humanity [. . .] particularly the proposition of Nestorius, the Bishop of Antioch,[26] who held that the Virgin did not bring forth the Son of God but a mere man. From such heresies the denial of other articles of the Christian faith may be implied without ever being directly affirmed. [. . .]

There is a third sort of heresy maintained by the Church of

Rome, which because it is still farther removed from the foundation of faith, might appear to be no threat to faith. But it is. Because of the weakness in the common person's ability to grasp conclusions that follow only from countless deductions from a principle, the repugnancy between these heresies and the foundation of faith is not readily apparent. There is this sort of heresy in the subtlety of arguments by the Roman Church when she teaches her doctrine of works.

What person is there who would refuse to subscribe to the basic words of this doctrine? Could such a person directly deny and grant the same thing? Our own proceedings in disputing the idea of meritorious works shows not only that the Romanists hold, but also that we acknowledge them to hold, to the foundation of faith, notwithstanding their opinion about works. We do not have to argue with them that Christ alone has satisfied and appeased His Father's wrath and that Christ alone merited salvation. We should do well in these disputes if we did not try to prevail by groaning over positions we know they do not hold and are quite assured they would never permit.

The answers of those in the Roman Church to all the arguments brought against them in this controversy do not allow us to doubt whether or not they hold the foundation. Can anyone who has read their books be ignorant of how they frame their answers to this issue? They say that the remission of all our sins, the pardon of whatever punishment we may deserve, the rewards that God has laid up for us in heaven are all purchased and obtained for us by the blood of our Lord Jesus Christ. They affirm also that Christ's grace applies to no particular case except by such means as God may have appointed and even then such means are as dead instruments unless they are enlivened and made efficacious by the blood of Christ.

Finally, the Romanists hold that, since grace is purchased for us by the blood of Christ and freely bestowed on us without any merit on our part, the good things which we do when grace is received are made meritorious only by that grace.

Some of these statements of theirs I ask you to accept on my authority. If you want to hear other authorities, here are a few.

[Hooker now cites two Roman Catholic writers: Luis of Granada, a sixteenth-century Spanish theologian, and Francis Panigorla, aka Jean Tonsi (1528–94), the Bishop of Asti.]

If anyone thinks that I seek to varnish the Catholic position in order to put a better foot on a lame cause, let him know that ever since I first began to understand the Roman meaning in these matters, I have found their ambiguity greater than they themselves – knowing not the guile of Satan – are, perhaps, aware of. Their apparent ignorance of the danger of their doctrine is sufficient proof that they are not directly denying the faith. Yet if there were no other leaven in the whole lump of their doctrine, this would be sufficient proof that their belief in this matter is not in agreement with the fundamentals of Christian faith.

The Pelagians, always better friends of nature than of grace, made themselves enemies of grace by all their shouting to the effect that we have our souls, and all the faculties related to our souls, as well as our free will and all of its power, directly from God. And is not the Church of Rome an adversary to the belief in Christ's singular merits when it claims that we have received through the blood of Christ the power of earning salvation by our merits? Sir Thomas More set down the differences between us and Rome in this matter when he said that one is required to do good works if one has the time and means, and that when such works result from true faith one will be rewarded. [. . .] I can see by this argument of Sir Thomas More how easy it is even for men of great capacity and judgement to mistake what is written and spoken on one side of an issue and another. As he saw it, Roman doctrine made the works of man rewardable in the next world through the goodness of God, whom it pleased to set great store on our poor deeds. Our view, on the other hand, is that a person receives his eternal and high reward not because of any work of his but for his faith alone for the sake of which he does good works. Our doctrine was learned at the feet of Christ Who taught that God justifies the believing person not for the worthiness of his faith but for the worthiness of Him who is believed.[27]

God abundantly rewards everyone who does good works, not

for any value in the works, but solely because of His mercy. The Roman position is that, as pure water has no taste in itself but when it passes through a sweetened pipe it takes on the pleasant odour of the pipe, so our works satisfy God for our sins and earn us merit once we have received God's grace. If we commit no mortal sin or heinous crime on which to spend the credits we have earned with God, then they may be credited to the account of whomever the priests in the house of God are pleased to bestow them. In this way, we may offer God satisfaction for our own sins and those of others. [. . .]

— *Grace* —

If it were not such a strong delusion which has taken possession of their hearts, is it not possible that the Romans would see how plainly they gainsay the very grounds of the Apostolic faith? Isn't this the salvation by grace which is mentioned so often in the sacred Scriptures of God? By grace we are saved, the Apostle said, and by grace, as a gift – something that comes not of our doing or nature, lest anyone should boast and say, 'I have effected my own salvation.' By grace, the Romans also say – but they mean a sort of grace by means of which those who wear the heavenly diadem wear only what they have won for themselves. As if he had foreseen how the Roman Church would one day abuse the world with such ambiguity of language, the Apostle declared what is meant by grace as the cause of salvation: 'He saved us according to his mercy.'[28] [. . .]

It is repugnant to say that we are saved by the worthiness of our actions. In so saying we deny the grace of our Lord Jesus Christ, we debase, annul, and annihilate the benefit of His bitter passion, if we rest in the proud imagination that life everlasting is deservedly ours, that we merit it, that we are worthy of it.

However, consider how many virtuous and just men, how many Saints, how many martyrs, how many ancient Fathers of the Church, held various perilous opinions, among them the hope that they might make God a party to efforts to atone for their sins by voluntary acts of penance which they laid upon themselves. Are we to conclude that, because such opinions were injurious to Christ, we must hurl deadly epitaphs at these men and declare them damned in their graves, or that there is no salvation for them because they denied directly the foundation of faith? [. . .] Unless we allow for a distinction between those who err and those who obstinately persist in error, how is it possible that anyone may ever hope to be saved? If I thought that, I would have no hope for any person living or dead.

— *Salvation for the Pope* —

Give me a person of whatever estate or condition, yes, even a cardinal or a pope, who in his most extreme affliction comes to know himself and whose heart at the end of his life God has touched with sorrow for his sins and filled with love of Christ's Gospel, and whose eyes God has opened to the truth, and whose mouth He has opened to renounce all heresy and error except for this one opinion, that God requires good works of him. He is fallible and he trembles and is discouraged. Yet he might yield and be recalled from this great error if I, and others like me, were only more wise and skilful in both old and new knowledge. Am I to think that because of this single error such a person cannot so much as touch the hem of Christ's garment? Should I not, in such a case, hope that Christ's virtue might save him? Because his error indirectly overthrows the foundation of faith, shall I cast him out as one who has cast off Christ, as one who holds to Christ by not even a slender thread? No.

I will not be afraid to say even to a cardinal or a pope in this plight, 'Be of good comfort. Ours is a merciful God.' Ours is a God who makes the most of what little faith we have, not a capricious sophister who gathers up the worst of our mistakes.

Is there any reason why I should be held suspect or that you should be offended by my words on this subject? Set aside our mutual affection and let the matter be considered objectively. Is it really dangerous to imagine that such men may find mercy from God? The hour may come when we shall think it a blessed thing to hear that if our sins were like those of the popes and cardinals, the bowels of God's mercy are as large.

I am not talking here about a pope with an emperor's neck under his foot or a cardinal riding his horse up to the bridle in the blood of Saints, but a pope or a cardinal sorrowfully penitent, stripped of usurped powers, delivered and recalled from error, an Antichrist converted and lying prostrate at the feet of Christ. Shall I think that Christ would spurn such a man? Shall I contradict and deny the merciful purposes of God made to all penitent sinners by excepting the name of pope or cardinal? What difference in the world is there between a pope and a cardinal and a John Doe in a case like this?

Let it be granted that it is impossible for popes and cardinals, once they have come to such high rank in the Church, to be touched by such remorse. [. . .] Assume even that it is as likely that St Paul or an angel should preach heresy as that a pope or cardinal should admit the truth in this matter of faith and works. Still, I ask, 'What do we find in their persons that excludes them from salvation?' You answer that it is not their persons but the error they commit about works that denies them God's mercy. But what if they hold this erroneous doctrine and yet soundly and sincerely maintain all other parts of the Christian faith? What if they have to some degree all the virtues and graces of the Holy Spirit and all other tokens of God's elected children within them except for this one matter concerning works? What if they are so far from having any proud presumptions that they should be saved because of the worthiness of their good deeds? Suppose they are troubled, molested, and somewhat dejected by too great a fear, which rises out of an erroneous idea that God will require some goodness in them, which they find lacking in themselves. What if they hold this opinion solely as an error and are not obstinate in this persuasion but would be glad to forsake it if they could find even one reason sufficient to disprove it? What if the only bar to their forsaking this error before they die is their ignorance of the means to disprove it? What if the reason why such ignorance is not removed is a lack of knowledge?

Let me die if ever it is proved that simple error in such a case excludes a pope or a cardinal from all hope of eternal life. Surely I must confess to you that, if it be an error to think that God may be merciful to save men even when they err, then my greatest comfort is my error. Were it not for the love I bear to this error, I would neither wish to speak nor to live.[29]

Now I return to the mother sentence, which I never thought would produce so much trouble: 'I doubt not but God was merciful to save thousands of our fathers living in popish superstition, inasmuch as they sinned out of ignorance.' Alas, what bloody matter is contained in this sentence that it should be an occasion for so many harsh censures? Did I say that thousands of our ancestors in the Roman Church might be saved?

I did, and I showed as well how this could happen. I cannot deny it. Did I say that I doubt not that they were in fact saved? I see no impiety in this opinion even if I had had no reason in the world to hold it. Did I say that their ignorance made me hope that they found mercy and so were saved? Yes. For what hinders salvation but sin? Sins are not equal, and although ignorance does not abolish sin, it does make it a lesser sin and gives us greater hope that our forefathers in the Roman Church may have found eternal life. We most pity – and I do not doubt that God has the greatest compassion for – those who sin out of a lack of understanding.

Sundry others have expressed this opinion in much the same words as I have used here. It is my misfortune that the same sentences which support this truth in other men's books, are seen as supporting heresy when I recite them. If I am deceived on this point, it is not the papists who have deceived me but the blessed Apostle, St Paul. What I have said of others he said of himself when he wrote, 'I obtained mercy for I did it ignorantly.'[30] Properly construe his words and you cannot misconstrue mine. I speak no differently from him, and my meaning is the same as his.

Thus I bring the question concerning our fathers in the Church of Rome to an end. I had spoken of this matter earlier when a suitable occasion to do so had presented itself, in order to assess the weighty cases of the separation between the Church of Rome and us. I had made particular reference to the weak motives of those who remain in that Church. At that time I saw fit to utter that fateful sentence concerning their possible salvation in order that all might understand how unfairly we are accused of condemning those who lived before our time and held different opinions than we do. More than this one sentence I had not thought it wise to utter, judging it better to examine our own estate than to sift through what has become of others. I was afraid that by wading too far into such questions I might seem worthy of that rebuke which our Saviour thought necessary, in a case not unlike this one, when He said, 'What is this to you?'[31]

When I was forced, contrary to my expectation, to justify my words, I could not but yield to the entreaties of others to proceed with a fuller satisfaction on this subject. I have walked into this subject with both reverence and fear: reverence toward our fathers who lived in former times, fear when I consider those who are still alive.

I am not ignorant of how ready men are to nourish and soothe themselves with evil. Shall I, like the person who loves this world more than Christ, incur the high displeasure of the mighty of the earth? Shall I hazard my goods, endanger my standing, even put my life in jeopardy rather than yield to that error which so many of my ancestors embraced and still found favour in the sight of God? [. . .] If I should fail to help the Lord against the mighty of the earth and instead help the mighty against the Lord, I might justly fall under the burden of the curse laid upon those who deny the Lord. But if the doctrine I teach is a flower gathered from the garden of the Lord, a part of the saving truth of the Gospel – even if poisonous creatures suck venom from it – I might wish that things were otherwise but can content myself with my lot, in part, because I am not alone in what has befallen me.

St Paul preached a comfortable truth when he taught that the greater the misery of our iniquities the readier the mercy of the Lord, if we will but seek Him out. The more we have sinned the more glory and praise and honour to Him who pardons our sin. Only mark what obscene conclusions are drawn by some from the Apostle's words. [. . .] He was accused of teaching whatever his opponents said they gathered from his teaching, even though what they said was not only tangential to but actually contrary to his meaning. The Apostle says that the condemnation of those who do this is just.

I am not eager to speak words of condemnation. From my heart, I wish for the conversion of those [radical Calvinists] who perversely interpret my words. But I must say that those who harden themselves and still presume that God's mercy toward others will apply to them have a fearful case. It is true that God is merciful, but let us beware of the sins of presumption. Because God delivered Jonah from the depths of the sea, will you cast yourself headlong from the cliffs and say in your hearts, 'God will deliver us'? God pities the blind who long to see but will God pity him who could see but hardens himself with blindness? No! Christ has revealed too much to you for you to claim the privilege of ignorance that may have saved your forefathers.

— *Toleration* —

As for those of who have examined this issue of the condition of our forefathers in the Church of Rome, or any other matter we may put before you, a good rule for you to follow is to stand fast in your own best understanding of the way of the Lord and then speak out in a peaceful and righteous manner. Just as a loose tooth causes great grief to a person who tries to eat, so is a loose and unstable word in speech, which is intended to instruct others, offensive. 'Shall a wise man speak words of the wind,' light, inconsistent, unstable words? asks Eliphaz. Surely even the wisest may sometimes speak 'words of the wind'. [32]

Such is the perverse constitution of our nature that we neither understand perfectly the way of the Lord, nor steadfastly embrace it when it is understood, nor graciously utter it when it is embraced, nor peaceably maintain it when it is preached. The best of us is overtaken, sometimes by blindness, sometimes by hastiness, sometimes by impatience, sometimes by other passions of the mind to which, as God knows, we are subject. We must, therefore, be content to pardon others and crave their pardon in all such matters. Let no one think himself free from mistakes and oversights in his speech.

What I have said to you on this subject is, I hope, sound doctrine. Even if my words have seemed otherwise to some persons at whose hands if I have received injury, I willingly forget it. Considering the benefit I have reaped by the deeper search for truth required by this criticism, I am inclined to the view of the Apostle when he said, 'They have not injured me at all.'[33] I wish my critics as many blessings in the kingdom of heaven as the words and syllables they have forced me to utter in this matter.

I could not have been more sparing in speech than I have been. St Jerome said, 'It becomes no one to be patient about the crime of heresy.' To the contrary, I think we should always be patient even when the crime of heresy is intentional. Silent I could not be, my beloved, in a matter of such consequence, especially when the love I bear to the truth in Christ Jesus was called into question. Therefore, I beseech those who started this dispute [especially Walter Travers, Reader at the Temple Church] to remember, in the spirit of Christ's meekness, that a watchman may cry 'enemy' when it is, indeed, a friend who approaches. For my part, since a watchman is not more worthy to be loved for his alertness than disliked for his mistakes, I have decided, in so far as I am able, to remove all suspicion of unfriendly intention or false meaning on the part of my critics. God knows my heart is free of such ill will.

Now to you, my beloved, who have listened to all of this, I have no further words of admonition than those offered to me by St James when he said, 'My brethren, do not have the same faith in persons that you have in our glorious Lord Jesus.' You must learn that it is not in itself harmful, neither should it be scandalous, nor offensive, if, in cases where there is doubt about doctrine, we listen to the differing opinions of others. Caiaphas may have one interpretation and Apollos another. Paul is of this mind and Barnabas of that. If this offends you, the fault is your own. Maintain peaceable minds and you may find comfort even in this variety of opinion.[34]

Now the God of peace give you peaceable minds and turn them to your everlasting comfort.

Notes

1. Although traditionally incorporated as part of the sermon called *A Learned Discourse of Justification, Works, and How the Foundation of Faith is Overthrown*, this is probably a separate tractate delivered at about the same time as the earlier sermon which I have called 'Grace and Righteousness'. The subject matter here focuses on the highly controversial issue of salvation for Roman Catholics, but the general issue of faith versus works remains as the central theme. Hooker's remarks in this sermon may have cost him further advancement in the Church hierarchy. He was too moderate toward the hated papists. See headnote to 'Grace and Righteousness' and my *Richard Hooker Prophet of Anglicanism* (Burns & Oates, Tunbridge Wells; The Anglican Book Centre, Toronto, 1999), 187–92.
2. Hebrews 1.2.
3. This is the specific statement that was thrown up in Hooker's face by such detractors as his principal antagonist at the Temple Church, Walter Travers, who virtually accused him of treason for making it. See Secor, *Richard Hooker*, 190–2.
4. Revelation 18.4; Matthew 24.16; Luke 21.21; Genesis 19.15.
5. Jude 1.22.
6. John 3.17–18; Revelation 2.21–23.
7. 1 Timothy 3.16; Matthew 16.16; John 1.49; 4.42.
8. Galatians 5.2; 3.1–4; 5.2–12.
9. Nestorius of Antioch (d. after 451) was made Patriarch of Constantinople in 431 but declared a heretic by the Roman Church for the doctrine that Christ is two distinct natures: divine and human. He was deposed by the Council of Ephesus in 436. Some, like the Calvinist Theodore Beza (1519–1605), saw the Lutheran doctrine of consubstantiation in the Eucharist as an embodiment of the Nestorian heresy.
10. Luke 13.3.
11. Psalms 19.12; 15.7.
12. 2 Thessalonians 2.10–12; Revelation 13.8.
13. Romans 4.8, 11, 22–24; James 2.21–24.
14. Hebrews 11.15; James 5.11; Matthew 22.35; Luke 11.51, 41.
15. The *Wittenberg Confession* (1552) was basic Lutheran doctrine. It was used in 1563 by the English Archbishop, Matthew Parker, as a partial basis for *The Thirty-Nine Articles*.

16. John 6.68; 2 Timothy 3.15.
17. Acts 16.17.
18. Mark 1.1.
19. Acts 25.18–19; 1 Corinthians 1.23; 2 Corinthians 6.15. For a discussion of Hooker's use in this paragraph of the Fathers and ancient philosophers, see W. Speed Hill, gen. ed., *The Folger Library Edition of the Works of Richard Hooker* Vols I–V (The Belknap Press of Harvard University, Cambridge, MA and London, 1977–1990), V, 741–2.
20. Romans 8.10; Philippians 2.16; Matthew 28.20; 1 Peter 1.23; 1 John 3.9; 5.12.
21. John 10.28.
22. Marcellus (d. *c.* 374) was the Bishop of Ancyra who was deposed for his idea that within the unity of God the Spirit and the Son emerged as independent beings only for the purposes of creation and redemption and then returned to the unity of the Godhead.
23. Philippians 3.2–3; Mark 10.16; Luke 15.20.
24. The Pelagian heresy, named after the fifth-century theologian, Pelagius, was that man, who was not doomed by original sin, could by an exercise of his free will do those good works that could earn him God's grace. The issue of free will has plagued Christian thinkers since at least the time of Augustine, Bishop of Hippo (354–430).
25. Zanchius, *Epistola ad Comitem*, *De Religione*, 1585, p. 3. Jerome Zanchius of Bergamo (1516–90) was a noted disciple of Calvin who advocated the doctrine of supralapsarianism (double predestination), which affirms that God predetermines some to salvation and others to damnation. While Hooker seems to have admired this theologian for some of his views, he was decidedly uncomfortable with the idea of predestination.
26. There has always been dispute about what Nestorius (d. after 451) actually believed. Hooker follows the practice among Catholics and Protestants alike of his day of crediting Nestorius with a wide variety of opinions of Eastern Orthodoxy thought to be heretical by Western Christians.
27. Thomas More (1478–1535) had a more moderate view on faith and works than Hooker credits here. The work cited is his *A Dialogue of Comfort Against Tribulation*, 1.12. See *Folger Edition*, V, 759–60.
28. Titus 3.5.
29. This statement reveals clearly Hooker's passion on the subject of tolerance for Catholics as well as the risk he ran in endangering his career over the issue. His opponents, as noted earlier, sought to discredit him over this and similar comments in this sermon. See Secor, *Richard Hooker*, 188–93.
30. 1 Timothy 1.13.
31. John 21.22.
32. Eliphaz was one of Job's questioners. Job 15.2.
33. Galatians 4.12.
34. James 2.1; 1 Corinthians 3.4–6.